Legend (inset, upper left):

1 CLACKMANNAN
2 DUNBARTON
3 FLINTSHIRE
4 KINROSS
5 LONDON
6 MIDDLESEX
7 MIDLOTHIAN
8 PEEBLES
9 RENFREW
10 RUTLANDSHIRE
11 SOKE OF PETERBOROUGH
12 WEST LOTHIAN

DOGGER

BANK

60—120 Ft.

ATLANTIC OCEAN

ICELAND
Saudhárkrókur
Eskifjördhur
Mt. Hekla (Vol.) 4747
Vik

LANGANES

Arctic Circle

THE FAEROES (Den.)
Thorshavn

SHETLAND IS. (Scot.)
Lerwick

ORKNEY IS.

HEBRIDES
The Minch
SCOTLAND
Moray Firth
GRAMPIANS
Aberdeen
Dundee
GLASGOW
Firth of Forth
Edinburgh
BRITISH
NORTHERN IRELAND
Belfast
ISLES
CHEVIOT HILLS
NEWCASTLE-ON-TYNE
KINGDOM
Carlisle
IRELAND
Galway
IRISH SEA
LIVERPOOL
LEEDS
Hull
Dublin
MANCHESTER
Leicester
Cork
Cobh (Queenstown)
CAPE CLEAR
St. George's Chan.
BIRMINGHAM
AMSTERDAM
NETHERLANDS
The Hague
Southampton
Portsmouth
LONDON
Thames
The Thames
Dover
BELGIUM
LANDS END
SCILLY IS.
English Channel
Cherbourg
CHANNEL IS. (Br.)
Le Havre
Rouen
Str. of Calais
Lille
BRUSSELS
Luxembourg
LUX.
Brest
Rennes
PARIS
Reims
Orléans
St. Nazaire
Nantes
Tours
Dijon
FRANCE
Loire
La Rochelle
Gironde
Bay of Biscay
Bordeaux
Dordogne
MASSIF CENTRAL
Clermont-Ferrand
Lyons
Mont Blanc 15 781
Garonne
Nîmes
Toulouse
PYRENEES
Marseilles
Gulf of Lions
Toulon
Bayonne
Pico de Aneto 11 168
Ebro
ANDORRA
El Ferrol
La Coruña
C. DE FINISTERRE
Gijón
Oviedo
Santander
S. Sebastián
Bilbao
CORD. CANTABRICA
Vigo
Oporto
PORTUGAL
Douro
Valladolid
Salamanca
SIERRA DE GUADARRAMA
Zaragoza
BARCELONA
Tarragona
Tortosa
Coimbra
Tagus
MADRID
SPAIN
LISBON
Guadiana
SIERRA MORENA
Valencia
BALEARIC ISLANDS (Sp.)
I. DE MENORCA
I. DE MALLORCA
Palma de Mallorca
I. DE IBIZA
C. DE LA NAO
Murcia
Cartagena
Guadalquivir
Seville
SIERRA NEVADA
Almería
Cádiz
Málaga
Gibraltar (Br.)
Ceuta (Sp.)
I. DEL ALBORAN (Sp.)
Oran
Straits of Gibraltar
Tangier
Tetuán
C. DE SAO VICENTE
Algiers
ALGERIA (Fr.)
Constantine
Sfax
Bone
Bizerte
Tunis
TUNISIA

NORWAY
Trondheim (Nidaros)
DOVRE FJELD
Galdhøpiggen 8400
Sogne Fjord
Bergen
Stavanger
Oslo
Kristiansand
LINDESNES
Skagerrak
Glomma
Lagen

SWEDEN
Ume
Umeå
Gulf of Bothnia
Vaasa
Gävle
Dal
Uppsala
STOCKHOLM
Norrköping
Karlstad
Lake Väner
Göteborg
Lake Vätter
GOTLAND
Visby
ÖLAND
BORNHOLM (Den.)

FINLAND
Luleå
Oulu
Turku
Hangö
Liyepaya
Klaypeda
Kaliningrad

DENMARK
Aalborg
COPENHAGEN
Malmö
Kattegat
Kiel
Lübeck
HAMBURG
Bremen
Hannover
Helgoland (Ger.)
Rügen
Szczecin
Gdańsk
Toruń
POLAND
Poznań
Wrocław
BERLIN
Magdeburg
GERMANY
ESSEN
COLOGNE
Leipzig
Dresden
Bonn
Rhine
Mainz
FRANKFURT
Nuremberg
STUTTGART
Oder
ERZGEBIRGE
BOHEMIAN FOREST
PRAGUE
CZECH.
Plzeň
M. Ostrava
Brno
Bratislava
SUDETES
MUNICH
Boden See
Danube
VIENNA
LIECHT.
AUSTRIA
Graz
Maribor
Ljubljana
Zagreb
Trieste
YUGO.
Zürich
Bern
Lausanne
Geneva
SWITZERLAND
TURIN
MILAN
Venice
Po
Genoa
La Spezia
Bologna
San Marino
Zadar
Split
Ancona
Leghorn
Florence
APENNINES
ITALY
ROME
NAPLES
M. Vesuvius (Vol.) 3842
Nice
Monaco
CORSICA (Fr.)
Ajaccio
SARDINIA (It.)
Cagliari
C. SPARTIVENTO
TYRRHENIAN SEA
Palermo
SICILY (It.)
Mt. Etna (Vol.) 10 868
Catania
Messina
C. BON
MALTA (Br.)
Bari
ADRIATIC SEA

NORTH SEA

Inset (left margin):

NORTH SEA
King's Lynn
Wensum
Norwich
NORFOLK
Great Yarmouth
Lowestoft
Newmarket
Waveney
SUFFOLK
Bury St. Edmunds
EAST SUFFOLK
Ipswich
Stour
Colchester
ESSEX
Harwich
Chelmsford
Southend-on-Sea
R. Thames
Sheerness
Margate
NORTH FORELAND
Gillingham
Ramsgate
KENT
Canterbury
Maidstone
Dover
Folkestone
Hastings
Bexhill
Eastbourne
Strait of Dover
Calais
Dunkirk
Ostend
FLANDERS
Ieper
St. Omer
Armentières
Boulogne-Sur-Mer
Béthune
Somme
Hesdin
Arras
St. Valery
Crécy
Abbeville
Le Tréport
FRANCE
Étaples

Longitude East of Greenwich 2°

COPYRIGHT BY
RAND McNALLY & COMPANY
MADE IN U.S.A.

5° Longitude West of Greenwich 0° Longitude East of Greenwich 5°

LIFE WORLD LIBRARY

BRITAIN

OTHER BOOKS BY THE EDITORS OF LIFE

LIFE Nature Library

LIFE Science Library

The LIFE History of the United States

LIFE Pictorial Atlas of the World
      with The Editors of Rand McNally

The Epic of Man

The Wonders of Life on Earth
      with Lincoln Barnett

The World We Live In
      with Lincoln Barnett

The World's Great Religions

LIFE's Picture History of Western Man

The LIFE Treasury of American Folklore

America's Arts and Skills

The Second World War
      with Winston S. Churchill

LIFE's Picture History of World War II

Picture Cook Book

LIFE Guide to Paris

LIFE WORLD LIBRARY

BRITAIN

by John Osborne

and The Editors of LIFE

A
STONEHENGE
BOOK

TIME INCORPORATED   NEW YORK

COVER: Otter hunters, dressed
in traditional costumes and gaiters,
follow their pack of hounds
across the rich, rolling fields of Devon.

ABOUT THE WRITER

John Osborne's close acquaintance with Britain and the British people, which is reflected in his interpretive text for this volume of the LIFE World Library, began during World War II when he served as a TIME Correspondent in London. After the war, from 1946 to 1948, he was Chief of the TIME-LIFE London Bureau, and in subsequent years he has returned to the island many times both for business and for pleasure. A Mississippian of English and Scottish ancestry, he is a recognized commentator on foreign affairs and international social and political events. Since 1948 he has been LIFE's Chief Editorial Writer, Senior TIME-LIFE Far Eastern Correspondent and a LIFE Staff Writer. Over the past two decades he has written numerous magazine articles on British personalities and problems.

Contents

TIME INC. BOOK DIVISION

EDITOR
Norman P. Ross

COPY DIRECTOR   ART DIRECTOR
William Jay Gold   *Edward A. Hamilton*

CHIEF OF RESEARCH
Beatrice T. Dobie

EDITORIAL STAFF FOR "BRITAIN"

EDITOR, LIFE WORLD LIBRARY	*Oliver E. Allen*
ASSISTANT TO THE EDITOR	*David S. Thomson*
DESIGNER	*Ben Schultz*
CHIEF RESEARCHER	*Grace Brynolson*
RESEARCHERS	*Monica Horne, Renée S. Pickèl, Danuta Dorozynski, Irene S. Ertugrul, Patricia Appel, Lois Cantor, Gwyneth Barger*
PICTURE RESEARCHERS	*Margaret K. Goldsmith, Joan T. Lynch*
ART ASSOCIATE	*Robert L. Young*
ART ASSISTANTS	*James D. Smith, Richard Forte*
COPY STAFF	*Marian Gordon Goldman, Rebecca Chaitin, Carol Henderson, Dolores A. Littles*
PUBLISHER	*Jerome S. Hardy*
GENERAL MANAGER	*John A. Watters*

LIFE MAGAZINE

EDITOR   MANAGING EDITOR   PUBLISHER
Edward K. Thompson   *George P. Hunt*   *C. D. Jackson*

The text for the chapters of this book was written by John Osborne, for the picture essays by Henry Moscow. The following individuals and departments of Time Inc. helped in producing the book: Alfred Eisenstaedt, Eliot Elisofon, Dmitri Kessel, Leonard McCombe, Carl Mydans and Howard Sochurek, LIFE staff photographers; Honor Balfour of the London Bureau; Rosalind Constable; Clara Applegate of the TIME-LIFE News Service; Doris O'Neil, Chief of the LIFE Picture Library; and Content Peckham, Chief of the Time Inc. Bureau of Editorial Reference. Much valuable research was done in London by Michael Demarest and by Maureen Snowball Green.

Introduction

To write an appropriate introduction to this volume on Britain is a formidable task, because the scope and character of John Osborne's work is formidable. I would expect from his pen and his mind an exceptional contribution to the LIFE World Library, for I learned during my almost four years in Britain to have a respect for his penetrating observations and interpretations of events as great as was my liking for him as a person.

Mr. Osborne has written of Britain and the British with a rare combination of realism, respect, affection and understanding. He covers in one small volume a panorama of the history of Britain from the days of the early Anglo-Saxons to the present moment. He gives us a view of the great "island empire"—the most extensive in the chronicles of the human race. He touches discriminatingly on the various facets of the crystal of the British story and the evolution of the Britain of today—its commerce, its art and literature, its education, its interesting and effective system of politics and government, which adapts the forms of monarchy to the substance of democracy. He describes the sociological influences that are mirrored in the British social, economic and political matrix. To achieve all this with a perspective as sensitive as it is wise is indeed a notable accomplishment.

Necessarily in such a small compass Mr. Osborne has omitted certain phases of Britain's evolution that others might have selected. He may also have exaggerated certain attitudes and the causes of them. But these minor flaws—if, indeed, they are flaws at all—are inevitable in such a short book covering such a long and complicated history. Certainly they do not detract from the notably high quality of Mr. Osborne's work.

If Britain is not today the dominant power it used to be, it is not only because in the present context of international politics, charged with the discordant notes of the cold war and marked by the migration of might both toward the New World and toward Eurasia, a purely national policeman can only rarely restrain and quell disorders in remote lands. It is also because waves of nationalism—sometimes violent, often inspired by designed treachery and calculated subversion—have taken a heavy toll of Britain's authority; and, too, it is because the ravages of two great convulsions in which Britain, on occasions, stood bravely alone have imposed weighty demands on the country's resources.

But no matter how great may have been the changes that have befallen Britain, and no matter how incompatible may appear to be the contradictory views held by some of the British people, Britain is a staunch and gallant ally which possesses, through long experience in world affairs, the talent, if not the military strength alone, to exert wholesome and beneficial influences on the world for longer than "the human eye can see."

LEWIS W. DOUGLAS
*former U.S. Ambassador
to the Court of St. James's*

1

A Country of Character

BRITAIN and its people possess a quality that is more durable than any of their empires, stronger than their Commonwealth, and more arresting to the world than their dwindling status as a great power. This quality is the British character.

Like so much else that is British, this character defies precise definition. It is, however, a tangible and living thing. The very words "the British" instantly conjure up among non-Britishers the image of a people, a nation and a national personality. Although the image varies from person to person, country to country and time to time, *some* image of Britain and of the British character is the common property of most of the people of the world.

Professor Brian Harrison, dean of the Faculty of Arts at the University of Hong Kong, may owe his life to the power of the British image in the mind of a Japanese officer. Harrison, a

Dublin Irishman who is also a loyal Briton, was captured with the British forces at Singapore in 1942. He risked a most unpleasant death when he refused to broadcast anti-British propaganda and thereby disproved his captors' assumption that all southern Irishmen hate the British. His attempts to explain his dual loyalty seemed to be bringing torture and a firing squad steadily closer. Suddenly a senior Japanese officer, who had sat silently by during Harrison's several interrogations, spoke up. "I understand," he said. "Let him go." Pondering this episode during the war years of captivity that followed, Harrison concluded that his Japanese savior had a fixed conception of how Britons should behave and was moved to compassion when an Irishman fulfilled it.

HOW the image may change with time and circumstance is illustrated by the case of India. Until 1947, when Britain freed India in one of the finest acts of statesmanship in history, the British image among Indians was that of the imperial regime—at once hated, resented, envied and admired. Now the hostility and envy are gone; the Indians are free to welcome the British as individual businessmen, teachers and engineers. More British civilians live in India today than were there at any time during the 190 years of British rule. There the image of Britain has changed for the better. The Irish, on the other hand, were once horribly oppressed by the British and only won their freedom after a bitter and bloody struggle. For this and many other reasons, the average Irishman's views of Britain have scarcely changed at all.

The world-wide impression that the British are a remarkably cohesive race, with highly distinctive characteristics, is no accident. The British have been cultivating it for centuries, and the British image in its various forms is largely of their own making. The image has been so successfully fashioned, in fact, that even when they depart from it the British seem to be conforming to it. Where they have been disliked, it is probably because at that time they chose to be disliked in order to be respected adequately.

Nothing could be more mistaken than the notion, which is part of the common British image, that they do not care a fig for other people's opinions of them. In their special way, the British care tremendously about what other people think of them.

A retired colonel of the British army, an Englishman complete with a tight face and a gray mustache, demonstrated this important truth to an American visitor in 1960. The colonel and the American met by chance one midnight in Edinburgh, in the lounge of the Caledonian Hotel, where Scotland's limitations upon the hours when liquor may be served do not apply to registered guests. When the American remarked that, among other things, he was studying the British character, the colonel became instantly alert. Just how, he inquired, did the American propose to describe that character? The American said that such adjectives as "durable," "decent," "aloof," "modest," "proud," "shy" and "stubborn" came to mind, adding for mild provocation the classic French judgment that the British are inherently "perfidious."

The colonel ignored the reference to the famous epithet, "perfidious Albion" ("Albion" is an old literary name for England). "*Stubborn*, did you say?" he growled. "I shouldn't say that we're stubborn. We do change, you know. Surely there's a better word for us?" Desiring to pacify the agitated colonel, the American suggested that "steady" might be acceptable. The colonel picked up his glass, downed a generous portion of whisky and said with the greatest satisfaction, "Steady—that's it! That's the word! Yes, I'd agree with you if you said that we're steady."

NOT everything that Britons do and say is consciously calculated to have a certain effect, of course. But, somehow or other, much that they do and say has a desirable if not specifically desired effect. An amusing example is the way in which their endless preoccupation with the famous British climate serves to sustain two useful impressions: first, that people who can endure British weather can endure and accomplish anything; and second, that people who enshrine a disagreeable combination of cloud, mist, fog, moderate temperatures and immoderate rain among their national glories, as the British do, are capable of any conceivable oddity of behavior and attitude. And the British do like to be thought odd—in respectable ways.

Julius Caesar, who came to England in 55 B.C., was impressed by the British climate. Another Roman, Tacitus the historian, wrote in the first century of the Christian era that Britain's "sky is overcast, with continual rain and cloud." G. M. Trevelyan, a modern British historian, recounted the early fame of British weather with marked satisfaction in his *History of England*, and in a very British footnote he observed: "The rapid changes of weather and temperature in Britain, a source of bitter merriment to its inhabitants in every age, stimulate the physical and mental energies and 'make us Englishmen.' " Sir Ernest Barker, editor of an anthology entitled *The Character of England*, quoted in his book the solemn assertion, ". . . the thin film of indistinct grey which on most days takes off the sharp edge of the English landscape . . . seems to have its parallel in English thought, which allows a margin of imprecision where accommodation and compromise are possible."

Guests in British hotels must be prepared at all times to discuss the shocking weather of the day with the hired help and to agree that any fair interludes are departures from the 'orrible norm. The British government's official handbook opens a substantial section on the subject with the heretical statement that "Britain has a temperate and equable climate," but reverts to orthodoxy with a gloomy note on the paucity of sunlight and a demure admission that "a period of as long as three weeks without rain is exceptional, and is usually confined to limited areas."

ONE thing about the peculiar British weather that makes it so dear to Britons is that it is *island* weather. The fact that they are islanders is immensely important and interesting to them, and it accounts for some of their most pronounced characteristics. So, at least, their

bards and historians have always asserted. Sir Winston Churchill bespeaks a profound British emotion when he lovingly calls Britain's annals "our long island history." A brief look at the island itself may therefore reveal further clues to the British character.

Britain—the name probably derives from that of an early Celtic tribe—consists of the three formerly separate countries of England, Scotland and Wales. Since 1707, when Scotland and England joined in an Act of Union (Wales had been formally incorporated in 1535), the island has been officially known as Great Britain. With Northern Ireland the unit is known politically as the United Kingdom of Great Britain and Northern Ireland. Counting the 186 islands and islets that lie off Scotland, there are actually several hundred inhabited British Isles, but of these Great Britain, or Britain, is by far the largest, being indeed the biggest island in all Europe. It is 300 miles across at its widest, and 600 miles long at its longest—all the way, as is traditionally said, from Land's End at the southwestern tip of Cornwall to the tiny locality of John o' Groat's near the northernmost point of mainland Scotland. With 52,675,556 individuals inhabiting its 94,214 square miles of land at last estimate (1961), it is the fourth most densely populated national land area in the world.

BUT Scotland, the land of Robert the Bruce, Robert Burns, haggis, tartans, bagpipes, porridge and Scotch whisky, has only 5.2 million people on its 30,411 square miles, or 171 per square mile, compared with 559 for Britain as a whole. It is made up of islands, mountains lost in cloud, wild moorlands, narrow valleys and meadowed plains. One third of its people live in or near its capital city, Edinburgh, and its fearsomely crowded manufacturing center, Glasgow. In the Highlands of the western and northern sections, the traveler may motor for hours without seeing another person. Technically Scotland is a distinct country with its own established (Presbyterian) church, its own systems of education and law and a tenacious survival of its ancient language (about 77,000

Scotsmen still speak Gaelic, and in a few remote Highland glens and on some offshore islands the natives speak nothing else). But its government is run from London, under a Secretary of State for Scotland who is usually a Scot, and although defiant Scottish nationalists claim that their land should break off from England and resume full nationhood, these demands sound empty even in proud Edinburgh.

SCOTSMEN still quote the promise of the men of Robert the Bruce in 1320, in the magnificent Declaration of Arbroath: "For so long as one hundred men of us remain we shall never submit under any conditions to the domination of the English." But for most Scots the old defiance has dwindled until it is little more than a well-preserved habit of blaming England for Scotland's many ills. And the characteristic sound of modern Scotland is not the crunch of claymores against English skulls; it is the gentle burr of Scotsmen calling English and American capital and factories to the new industrial towns that are currently rising or planned all over the lovely land.

The smallest of Britain's three "countries" is Wales, on the southwestern coast. Most of its 2.6 million people live in the coastal plains, in the deep green valleys and in the coal-mining and industrial areas of south Wales. But its harshly beautiful mountains and lonely uplands are the keys to its character: there the Welsh fought for centuries to preserve themselves and their Celtic culture from successive conquerors and molders from England. And there, in the process, they developed a xenophobic nationalism that still survives.

Well over half a million Welshmen speak the native Welsh, a mellifluous but (to outsiders) impenetrable variation of ancient Celtic. Many Welshmen assume as a matter of course that God converses in Welsh, but in Wales as a whole English is the prevalent language. It is used to denounce the English, to demand full independence for Wales, to contest for election to the British Parliament and to acknowledge a rather grudging pride in the fact that male heirs to the British throne are styled Prince of Wales —a custom which the British instituted in 1301 to placate their newly conquered Welsh subjects. "Wales" is derived from the Anglo-Saxon word for "foreigners" and was conferred upon the country by the English. The national name is "Cymru," meaning "countryman" or "friend."

A Welsh journalist, describing a community of "true" or Welsh-speaking Welsh, has attributed to them "acute non-conformity, a keen political sense, idealism, good humor and wit, a fondness for beer or religion and rugby football, a slight paranoia . . . a desire to talk and talk, a charm so winning that you might think them always in the right." The same source, however, concedes that other observers feel "they are bigoted, anarchistic, undisciplined, hypocritical, too fond of talking, too little fond of working."

The core of Britain is England, where some 43.5 million of the island's 51 million people live. England's heartland is in the south and southeast. There, to the east, are the low shores of East Anglia, where waves of early invaders from the European continent found easy landings and in the course of many centuries combined to evolve the people who became the English. There, to the south, are the higher but also accessible coasts that beckoned William the Conqueror's Normans across the English Channel from France in 1066 and so occasioned the final infusion of blood, custom and language which prepared the English to dominate all Britain and, in the course of time, to rule a fourth of the world.

SOUTHERN England is story-book England. It contains the white cliffs of Dover, a protruding wall of the chalk that underlies the undulant downs of Sussex and Kent; Canterbury and its majestic cathedral, where Geoffrey Chaucer's merrie pilgrims made their lighthearted worship and a famed archbishop, Thomas à Becket, was murdered; the swampy fens of Cambridgeshire where, to this day, farmers live in extreme isolation; Suffolk's dreaming villages and parish churches of time-weathered stone.

outwardly as they were four centuries ago.

There also are the universities of Oxford and Cambridge, where the English character of Britain has been nurtured and preserved since the 12th Century. There is great London, where the essence of southern England, of all England, and through them of all Britain is concentrated. And, beyond all else, there are the archetypes of the "meadows of England, shining in the rain." Swelling cities and spreading industry have impaired southern England's rural aspect, and as in all of Britain most of the people now live in towns or cities. But the area remains largely rural in look and tone.

On the island's southwestern peninsula are the Royal Duchy of Cornwall and the county of Devon, part of England but remote from it. The natives of Cornwall—a place of rocky cliffs, deep rain-soaked valleys and wild brown uplands—still speak of the rest of England as another place "out there." Devon is known for the grim wasteland of Dartmoor and the thick accents of the people.

A SHORT journey to the northeast by car, but a planet away in spirit, are the industrial Midlands, and beyond lies the north of England, varied economically and geographically. Britain's and the world's Industrial Revolution of the 18th and 19th Centuries was born there. Poet William Blake's "dark, Satanic mills" that enriched the region's businessmen and stained its landscape still darken such cities as Birmingham, Stoke-on-Trent, Manchester, the port of Liverpool and Yorkshire's drab cities: Bradford, Leeds and Hull. As new, modern factories and whole new factory towns spring up around the old cities, lovers of "England's green and pleasant land" (another Blake phrase) complain that the quiet countryside is vanishing with the urban explosion. But even the industrialized north has always had its fields, its moorlands and (in the Lake District celebrated in the poems of William Wordsworth) its sweet inland waters, and they still please the eye.

A FOURTH "country," Northern Ireland, considers itself extremely British indeed even though 75 miles of rough water separate it from Britain. The majority of its 1.4 million people are Protestant, heirs of the Presbyterian Scotsmen and Anglican Englishmen who settled in the old province of Ulster three centuries ago. Subsequent political and economic developments accentuated the differences between the island's north and south, and when Ireland was granted self-rule early in this century the Ulstermen violently objected to being included in the new state. Ever since then they have fought against severance from Britain, a status which for them would mean subordination to Roman Catholic southern Ireland.

The region's one big city, the shipbuilding and manufacturing center of Belfast, is closer economically and spiritually to Liverpool and Glasgow than it is to Dublin. Northern Ireland

---

SOME DIALECTS OF THE BRITISH ISLES

For numerous social and historical reasons, Britons express themselves in a wide variety of local dialects. Often the inhabitants of two villages only 10 miles apart will have quite different forms of speech. The phrases shown below are reproduced as the people in various regions of the British Isles would say them.

STANDARD ENGLISH	The young lady coming from the school over there, beyond the cowshed.
COCKNEY	The little kid comin' from the skule over thar pas' the kar shed.
NORTHERN IRELAND	The wee gurl coming frae the school yonder past the byre.
SCOTLAND (LOWLANDS)	Yon wee lassie coming frae the skuel yonder doon past the byre.
YORKSHIRE	Latle girl kumin frad skiewl yonder past cow house.
NORFOLK	Tha little moither a comin from tha shewel yin way, parst that bullock lodge.
CORNWALL	Li'l maid coming home vrum skule down there, past the shippen.

has its own Parliament for local affairs, and its own governor as well, but as a part of "the United Kingdom of Great Britain and Northern Ireland" it is subject to the British Parliament (to which it sends representatives) and the British Crown. Except for its pro-southern Catholic minority, it wants to stay that way.

ENGLAND and the English are so dominant in their island realm that they are often equated with Britain and the British. "I'm going to *England*," travelers say. The "nation of shopkeepers" to which Napoleon referred contemptuously (before it ended his career at Waterloo) was England. At the Battle of Trafalgar, it was England that expected every man to do his duty. The "bastard king" of the old ballad was England's king. In the World War II song, it is England that will always be. Histories of Britain turn out to be the *History of England* (G. M. Trevelyan) and *The Story of England* (Sir Arthur Bryant). Outraged Scots and Welshmen put this habit down to English arrogance and foreign ignorance, but it reflects the real balance of island forces. William Shakespeare was on the side of history, if not of strict accuracy, four centuries ago when he wrote immortally of "this scepter'd isle . . . this precious stone set in the silver sea . . . this England," while referring geographically to the whole of Britain.

The British character, in effect, is fundamentally the English character—though the Scots, the Welsh and the Irish have provided some of the most distinguished exemplars of that character. The Duke of Wellington and George Bernard Shaw were Irish; the great World War I prime minister, David Lloyd George, and the late poet, Dylan Thomas, were Welsh; Harold Macmillan, prime minister in the early 1960s, is a diluted Scot. They have all brought to the life and tone of English Britain a strength derived from difference, and this is a boon to a people who, for all of their internal differences, have a certain sameness in total aspect. But in order to contribute, the minorities are forced to abandon their regional fastnesses and enter the mainstream of British life—that is to say, of English

life. There is still an element of truth in the acid remark of Dr. Samuel Johnson, the 18th Century English wit, that a Scotsman's noblest prospect "is the high road that leads him to England."

Perhaps the most trenchant thing to be said of the English character is that its basic qualities neither require nor bear much elaboration. The world knows full well that the English at their historic best are brave, resourceful, dependable —and *steady*. Their abhorrence of violent social upheaval, their genius for quiet change, their mystic love of outdoor games, their respect for public order and private freedom—these and a hundred kindred characteristics are so familiar that a lengthy recital of them would make the English out to be as dull as they sometimes like to seem.

BUT the English are most interesting, and also best revealed, in their manifold variations from these expected traits (or from what appears to be expected). An extraordinary aspect of these variations, real and seeming, is that they never bring into question the solid, universally recognized elements of the English character. For example, the English tendency to produce spectacular eccentrics and do them honor merely demonstrates the extreme normality of most Englishmen. The fact that a bygone British ambassador had a habit of dashing naked through the parks of certain capitals on full-moon nights never got wide circulation. If it had, it would have been amusing chiefly because of the widespread public impression that Englishmen clothe themselves with great care, particularly when they are anxious to appear casually dressed.

A great deal of English writing about the English suggests that, although they enjoy an entrenched reputation for modesty and for self-deprecation, they have an equally entrenched feeling of self-admiration. Sir Thomas Browne, the 17th Century physician and philosopher, attributed to "the true Heroic English Gentleman" a peerless capacity for "Bright Thoughts, clear Deeds, Constancy, Fidelity, Bounty and generous Honesty." The 19th Century novelist, William Makepeace Thackeray, stated the point fairly: "For a steady self-esteem, and indomitable confidence in our own courage, greatness, and magnanimity, who can compare with the Britons except their children across the Atlantic?" A minor contemporary of Thackeray named Eliza Cook caught the spirit of many paeans by her literary betters when she wrote:

'Tis a glorious charter, deny it who can,
That's breathed in the words, "I'm an Englishman."

Englishmen take a morose pride in such faults as they find in themselves. Thus Daniel Defoe in 1701 wrote of "that vain, ill-natured thing, an Englishman," and Jonathan Swift at about the same time wrote, "I find you are a true Englishman; you never know when you are well." Sydney Smith, the celebrated early 19th Century clergyman and writer, remarked, "What a pity it is that we have no amusements in England but vice and religion." A subsequent essayist, Sir Arthur Helps, described his countrymen as "sad hearted Anglo-Saxons—heavy eaters, hard thinkers, often given up to a peculiar melancholy of our own." To the writer Thomas Carlyle in 1843 the English were "the stupidest in speech, the wisest in action," and E. M. Forster, the contemporary novelist and short story writer, asserted that, "It is not that the Englishman can't feel—it is that he is afraid to feel."

THE foibles of his countrymen, however, do not in any way diminish the Englishman's love of country. The late W. R. Inge of St. Paul's Cathedral, who was called "the gloomy dean" for his melancholy view of 20th Century society, assured his countrymen, "Never, even when the storm-clouds appear blackest, have I been tempted to wish that I was other than an Englishman."

The note of vanity in the foregoing quotations is related to another facet of the English character, snobbery. There have been changes recently in the class system that produces and thrives upon English snobbery, and these will be discussed later; what concerns us here is the pride that Englishmen of all classes take in their snobbery. Whether they superficially regard it as a blessing or a curse, it is recognized at every social level as an institution which, if not peculiar to England, has been uniquely perfected in England. "Snobbery in England," a writer in London's *Times Literary Supplement* observed, "is more than a joke or a frame of mind, more even than a relic of dying orders. It is a phenomenon of such complexity and force that nearly all our lives are affected by it, and the essence of the state is spiced with its pungency . . . When the foreigner tries a hand at the game, the English connoisseur smiles a faint superior smile: across the water most snobbery seems simple stuff, provincial, amateurish, impotent."

IN his excellent *Life in Britain*, published in 1956, J. D. Scott described the country as "a snob's Elysium." He noted, "Of course snobbery exists everywhere," mentioning America and France, and then said with what can only be read as quiet pride, "British snobbery is at once more subtle and more earthy." A character in one of George Bernard Shaw's plays says, "The whole strength of England lies in the fact that the enormous majority of the English people are snobs." Shaw probably meant this to be satire, although he himself was an accomplished snob. Many Englishmen would have difficulty in finding the satire; they would accept it as a perfectly serious statement of an admirable fact.

It is often noted of Englishmen, by themselves and others, that they like to play the part of human sheep. An anonymous but unusually acute student of the English raised a small storm a few years ago by stating in *The Times Literary Supplement*, "This mild, beneficent, trustful creature, easily imposed upon, unmindful of injury, is a pose." The pose is effective, he said, because the Englishman sees himself "so thoroughly . . . in any part which he has assumed, that he frequently deceives not only himself but others." The writer continued, "The English are in fact a violent, savage race," notable for their "ruthlessness" and also given to "the English habit of buccaneering, of dropping honest work

15

and taking to simple, bluff, hearty plunder."

In evidence the writer cited the slaughter of the American Indians (the English never tire of recalling that they were the first settlers of the American colonies), the brutal conquest and repression of Ireland, the extermination of rabbits and aborigines in Australia, the Royal Air Force's major part in the burning of Hamburg during World War II. Englishmen of letters, smarting under this analysis, were convinced that the author could not be English, but have been unable to identify the culprit.

ORTHODOX Englishmen and their women display a compulsive need to be thought not only unskilled, but positively disinterested, in the overt arts of love. A London journalist, championing the British pub as an essentially male preserve, recently asserted that Englishmen as a rule really do not value the company of their women. Nearly a century and a half earlier, Lord Byron, who had a great reputation as an amorist, wrote of "our cloudy climate and our chilly women." Hippolyte Taine, a Frenchman who studied the English with fond perception nearly 100 years ago, supposed that within every Englishman there must be a monster of repressed desires, kept marvelously in control but ever in danger of breaking out.

An English proverb—"The English love, the French make love"—perfectly sums up the average Englishman's conviction that, while he is not immune to love, he is above making too great a thing of it. According to J. D. Scott, "It is true to say that Englishmen on the whole do not take that pleasure, that special pleasure, not specifically sexual yet tinged with sexual feeling, in the company of women, that Italians or Frenchmen take. . . . What English people want from the opposite sex is, characteristically, not romantic love, nor passion, nor coquetry, but companionship, loyalty, affection —in a word, friendship."

If this is indeed the emotional pattern of England, the departures from it are vast and continuous. Some Englishwomen with a claim to respectability hesitate to lunch with male companions, including their husbands, at certain smart London restaurants on Saturdays: it is too widely assumed that Saturday luncheon pairs will be heading for love right after coffee. A few years ago an American report on England caused roars of English laughter with its assumption that the couples to be seen lying on their backs in London parks, in broad daylight, were symptomatic of national laziness. In London and other English cities, a phenomenal amount of public smooching can be observed. Young Englishmen and their girls are intertwined, but not immovable, at all hours of the day and night— in alleys, on the sidewalks, on museum steps, against trees, in the occasional sunlight and in pouring rain.

This proclivity is not, as is commonly supposed, confined to the visibly lower classes. In recent years "strip clubs" have thrived in London; the customers of the "better" ones appear to be made up largely of middle-class businessmen, prototypes of the respectably subdued Englishman, postponing the nightly return to suburbia for a fast drink and a show of nude girls. The shows often include acts involving simulated whippings and other abnormalities, but one hears no objections from the audience that this form of behavior is un-English.

INDEED, for all their habit of generalizing about themselves, it may be seen that the English are a lively people, easily misinterpreted and somewhat given to misinterpreting themselves. It also should be apparent that they cannot be arbitrarily labeled. Yet mankind is not mistaken in its conviction that the British have —and demonstrate—a distinctive character. The single quality that most clearly marks it, and is most widely recognized, was set forth some 50 years ago in a London magazine, *The Spectator*. The line is flat and very true: "The British subject," it runs, "has a repute for not knowing when he is beaten." An indignant foreigner who said much the same thing about the British was Adolf Hitler, raging against their impenetrable obtuseness at the peak of his power and of their glory in the dark year of 1940.

Through the soft morning mist, a streak of sunlight touches a meadow with pale gold as horsemen canter their jumpers over the turf.

Landscape That Shapes a People

A small and thickly peopled country aclutter with cities, Britain nevertheless retains much of the gently glowing beauty that inspired poet Rudyard Kipling to write, "Our England is a garden." Not far from London and other cities, there are still rural regions, peaceful and beloved, where tranquil rivers flow, rolling meadows shine and castles and cathedrals sit serenely, as they do in the England of the storybooks. But there are also grim moors and abrupt hills, and the character of the British people is molded by both the quiet, secluded valleys and the steep crags.

17

In gray majesty the British Houses of Parliament stand in the heart of London, looking out on the tugs and barges anchored on the

Thames River. Westminster Abbey is at the far left, beside the 323-foot-tall Victoria Tower; the Clock Tower at right houses Big Ben.

HARDY MUDLARKERS risk their necks in a uniquely English sport, racing small cars up and down steep and slippery hillsides.

GENTEEL PUNTERS at Oxford (*right*) run into a morning traffic jam on the Cherwell after attending a dawn song concert.

A monument to the exuberant age of the Tudor monarchs that followed feudalism, Compton Wynyates rises beyond a garden of flowers,

sculptured yews and fruit trees. Begun in the 16th Century, it is one of the most sumptuous and beautiful country houses in all of England.

ANCIENT PUB, London's George and Vulture has flourished since 1600. Benjamin Franklin, in his days as a diplomat, sipped brandy and listened to the gossip here.

UNCHANGING FARE at Rule's (*opposite*), a gathering spot for London businessmen, includes steak and kidney pie, as it did in 1798 when the restaurant was founded.

Exemplifying the unity of the United Kingdom's components, the standard of Scotland flutters above the Queen and Prince Philip (on

platform) *as Highland bands march by at the Braemar Games. The festival originated in contests among the Scotsmen's Celtic forebears.*

TOSSING THE CABER (*opposite*), a 19-foot log weighing 120 pounds, a brawny Scot competes in the Braemar Games under the critical gaze of a tam-topped judge.

WATCHING HIS ARROW in the annual Grand Wardmote of the Woodmen of Arden, the Earl of Aylesford (Head Woodman) helps continue an event begun in 1785.

FINANCIAL HUB *of London is "the City," a mile-square enclave independent of the rest of the metropolis, where much of the world banks, borrows, trades, charters ships and buys insurance*

THE ELITE LOOK of the City is seen in the top hats and the formal suits of the area's brokers. The City shelters half a million people by day, only some 5,000 at night.

CITY PARKING LOT is jammed with the Rolls-Royces and Bentleys (*left*) which belong to the City's powerful brokers and bankers, currency traders and underwriters.

CITY PUB, a crowded bar in Throgmorton Street, is a habitual preserve of men who deal casually in billions. Here, over mugs of ale, financiers often transact their business. The ancient independence of the City is so zealously maintained that technically even the Queen may not enter the area without the Lord Mayor's leave.

CRUSADER KING, Richard Lion-Heart rides to battle at Westminster Palace. He was seldom in England, but his bravery made him a symbol of chivalry. He died in 1199.

2

Forging the Modern Nation

ALTHOUGH we think of Britain as an old country, it is young in man's annals. Four thousand years before its inhabitants emerged from tribal chaos, the Egyptians had reared an empire on the Nile. When Plato was creating a philosophical system 2,300 years ago, Britain was still a land of barbaric communities. When Christ died for a world already surfeited with vanished civilizations, head-hunting was still a practice among the island's tribesmen. Fifteen centuries of the Christian era had passed before England fully acquired the qualities of a nation and began to reach for world power. The island-wide country we know as Great Britain, or Britain, has been a legal entity less than 300 years. The British Empire attained its zenith, entered its decline and was transformed into a Commonwealth during the first half of our century.

But we are not in error when we think of Britain as an ancient country. What counts is the determining character of the country and its people. The British character began to take shape long before the British nation existed. It was this character that an American writer, Catherine Drinker Bowen, had in mind when —like so many others—she marveled at "that strange island, so close yet so remote, so like any country yet so unlike—called England."

A series of paradoxes mark the island story. The most appalling evils sometimes worked to the good of Britain. For example, the lengthy and bitter contest between the Roman Catholic Church and antipapal Christians for supremacy in Britain, sullied though it was by horrors of torture, maiming and burning, contributed materially both to the growth of nationhood and to the toleration which the British eventually came to practice. Feudal barons who brutally oppressed their enslaved serfs provided at the same time a necessary check upon the equally vital development of centralized power. Early Parliaments, their membership restricted to a narrow and often selfish aristocracy, nurtured British liberty by asserting their own rights, and thus founded the representative system that is Britain's pride. In this island of infinite contradiction, human bestiality at times coincided with the highest flights of the human spirit: a generation before Shakespeare wrote that mercy droppeth as the gentle rain from heaven and Spenser penned his *Faerie Queene*, royal ministers were not above personally stretching gentle ladies on the rack.

PERHAPS this pervasive note of what an English historian calls a "conflict in the national makeup" is only natural in a nation fused from so many different peoples. Among the first settlers were an assortment of Stone Age tribesmen who had originated in continental Europe, and who were adept at farming and husbandry. By slow stages they learned how to use copper and bronze. Later immigrants, whom we call Celts, came from east of the Rhine River to the British Isles, speaking languages that still survive in Wales, Scotland and Ireland. (The word "Britain" is thought to be derived from an early

Celtic tribal name.) The imperial Romans ruled Britain for three and a half centuries, but apart from the site of London and some fine roads, they left amazingly little trace. Viking Norsemen from Scandinavia and finally Normans from France, who were themselves descended from raiding Norsemen, invaded in their turn and stayed to become Englishmen and Britons.

BUT the people who gave England its name, its essential language and its fundamental character were the Angles, Saxons and their less numerous cousins, the Jutes, tribesmen from the forests of Germany and Denmark who are commonly grouped as the Anglo-Saxons. They had been noted on the continent for their ability in farming, their hatred of cities, their tender regard (as things went in that cruel age) for their women, and for their savagery as warriors.

The Anglo-Saxons had first come to Roman Britain as coastal raiders. When they realized around 450 A.D. that the collapse of imperial Rome had left the island defenseless, they arrived in greater numbers to occupy and settle the land, by force if necessary. These new invaders, being essentially agrarian, either demolished the walled towns of the Romans or left them desolate. A chronicler writing a century later described the carnage: "Every colony is levelled to the ground by the stroke of the battering ram. The inhabitants are slaughtered along with the guardians of their churches, priests and people alike, while the sword gleamed on every side and the flames crackled around."

Some of the survivors, Romanized descendants of the Celts and earlier peoples, fled to the uplands of Cornwall, Wales and Scotland and there held out against intermittent assault. It is to this circumstance, continuing for centuries, that Wales and Scotland owe their separate identities. Celtic heroes defending a segment of their territory against the Saxon hosts gave rise to the story of King Arthur and his Knights of the Round Table.

Ruthless enslavers and occupiers though they were, the Anglo-Saxons from the first displayed a strong sense of social organization. As they cleared the forests and drained the swamps, villages and towns revived to handle a growing trade in skins, wool and honey. Roman London, probably never wholly abandoned, gradually recovered its importance as a port and a center of commerce (although centuries were to pass before it was a capital). Tribal chieftains, each in his area lording it over a rudimentary feudal society of *eorls* and thanes (noblemen), freemen and enslaved serfs, established seven contending kingdoms—chief among them Kent and Wessex in the south, and Mercia and Northumbria in central and northern "Englaland."

In less than two centuries, the Angles, Saxons and Jutes evolved from their Germanic dialects a common language with words that may be recognized as "English" today (thus: *stān* for stone; *hām* for home). Only a few holy scholars could write, and their working language was Latin. Around the year 700 some of the laws of Wessex were inscribed in the common Anglo-Saxon, but in the Latin alphabet.

In the Eighth Century the greatest of early island scholars, the monk Baeda or Bede, wrote in Latin of "the English nation." In the same century King Offa II of Mercia styled himself *Rex totius Anglorum patriae*, or King of all the land of the English, although he ruled only one of several English kingdoms. But the first ruler who in spirit deserved the title of King of England was the immortal Alfred of Wessex, known as Alfred the Great. In his lifetime (849–c.899) he embodied the finest qualities of the English character.

IN an age that knew little mercy, Alfred was merciful to his defeated foes and kind to his own people. When only clerics knew how to read and write, he mastered Latin and personally directed the translation of a number of Latin works into the Anglo-Saxon (or Old English) that he called "the language we all know." By royal command he set his astonished nobles and freemen to "learning English letters." He imported foreign scholars and craftsmen, established monasteries and schools, and gathered about him a literate civil service of priests and scholars. "God Almighty be thanked, we now have teachers in office," he wrote. The famous *Anglo-Saxon Chronicle*, the oldest existing connected historical record in English, was begun during his reign.

But Alfred, a genius in war as in peace, spent much of his reign saving Wessex from the most terrible of Britain's invaders, the galley-borne Norse Vikings from Scandinavia. Alfred's rural forces, once reduced to a few followers hiding with him in a swamp, finally compelled his Danish enemies to leave Wessex in peace, and the invaders were confined to an area of northern and central England called the Danelaw.

ALFRED'S son, Edward the Elder, later conquered the Danelaw and thereby became the first King of a united England. During the next 100 years the vigorous, flamboyant, flaxen-haired Norsemen merged gradually with the Anglo-Saxons and ultimately came to be an asset to the nation. Around the end of the 10th Century a new wave of Danes entered England, and in 1016 the great though harsh young Cnut, or Canute, became King by the choice of the Witan, or nobles' council. But Canute had the wisdom to adapt himself to the customs of the nation and to govern by its laws.

The England to which Canute came was early England complete: a vivid mosaic of cruelty and gaiety, crudity and elegance, a fierce love of freedom and a savage readiness to enslave. The Englishmen of the 10th Century were (in Sir Arthur Bryant's words) "a hearty and ruddy-faced race, much given to feasting, drinking and sport. They were lovers of hunting, hawking and horse-racing, cock-fighting and bull-baiting, glee-singing, buffooning and tumbling." In monasteries restored by Alfred and his successors after the Viking devastation, Benedictine monks composed music, studied mathematics and taught scientific farming. English craftsmen worked superbly in imported ivory, gold, jeweled ornaments and church vestments. In Wessex, now merely an earldom but thanks to Alfred the richest area of England, princes and nobles wore bright silken mantles adorned with golden collars and garnet brooches and, in their colorfully decorated halls, drank from cow horns and wooden goblets trimmed with gold. It was mainly a rural land—owned by great lords, tenanted by lesser freemen and often worked by serfs. By the 11th Century there were about 70 towns with populations of up to 4,000, and in London, now becoming an important European as well as English trading center, 20,000 people lived in wooden houses.

UNDER "the holy but imbecile" Edward the Confessor, a pious weakling descended from Alfred's line, England soon became disunited and vulnerable to conquest. A great English national hero, Harold Godwin, the son of a powerful earl, succeeded the childless Confessor upon his death, but it was too late to save the country. Across the English Channel, Duke William of Normandy, who had a tenuous claim to England's throne, saw his chance and took it. His invading army of some 10,000 mounted Norman knights and foot soldiers armed with bows and crossbows defeated Harold's valiant but erratic infantry of axmen, spearmen, drafted peasants and a few bowmen near the English coastal hamlet of Hastings on October 14, 1066. It was to be the last successful military invasion of Britain. On Christmas Day, William the Conqueror was crowned King William I, and Anglo-Norman England was born.

For some time the two civilizations stood side by side, but no Anglo-Saxon king ever again ruled England. The Anglo-Saxon nobility was dispossessed and dispersed. There is still some doubt about the degree to which Anglo-Saxon culture continued to survive. French became the language of government and the aristocracy, Latin remained the language of learning and the written law, and for a time Anglo-Saxon English was spoken only among the lowly. However, the Norman conquerors were in time absorbed by the island just as the earlier Norsemen had been, while the influence of the French language, arms and manners left an indelible mark on English life and history. William's great work was that he succeeded in unifying and strengthening the country under a central government, while preserving the English institutions that dated back to the time of Alfred.

The English and British story after the Norman conquest falls into four fairly distinct periods. The first covers the molding of the nation in the 500 years between the Conqueror's arrival and the death of King Henry VIII. In the next 250 years—the second period—the island became Great Britain, the first empire developed, and the world-wide Industrial Revolution got its start in the British Isles. In the third period, from 1795 to the end of World War I, Britain and its second empire (re-established and vastly expanded after the loss of the American colonies) gave the world the relatively stable time of *Pax Britannica*, or British Peace. Then came the fourth and present period of transition and decline from predominant world power to what the British hopefully call "world influence." The first three periods, which will be discussed in this chapter, can best be understood in terms of the outstanding individuals and the evolving institutions that contributed importantly to the England and Britain that we know today. The fourth historical period will be examined separately in Chapter 3.

THE two institutions that have both shaped and reflected the national character more than any others are the monarchy and Parliament. At the start of the first period, William the Conqueror devoted his enormous energies to vesting public power in the Crown. He made himself owner of all the land in England, granting his Norman barons their huge holdings only as the king's tenants. He asserted and savagely enforced the king's right to levy taxes, administer justice and require military service of his subjects. But even so tireless and ruthless a king as William could not rule alone. To help him govern and to give his measures a semblance of order, he assembled the *Curia Regis*, or Royal Council, a group of leading barons and churchmen. The king, the barons and the churchmen gradually came to share the power in England, and through several centuries they waged a continuous contest among themselves over the possession and use of that power. In so doing, they evolved the institution of parliamentary government, which has served as a model for modern legislatures.

A decisive factor in the contest between king and council was money. Monarchs and their governments were theoretically expected to subsist entirely on the king's personal revenues. But as the cost of governments, armies and wars increased, successive kings had to turn to their councils for extra funds. Within two centuries of the Norman conquest, the councils had been broadened to include not only the mightiest barons and churchmen but lesser nobles and clergymen, knights from the counties and representatives of the shires and boroughs, where merchants and artificers were now accumulating taxable wealth. The Latin word *parliamentum*, meaning discussion or parley, was first applied to these gatherings in 1239.

BUT, as with jury duty today, the royal summons to Parliament was not always greeted with joy. Rural knights absconded to escape attendance, and a borough in Devon asserted its right *not* to be represented. Yet the parliamentary power grew, and it soon dawned on the members that they could exact concessions from kings in return for the money the monarchs demanded. By the middle of the 14th Century, Parliament had divided into a House of Lords for the barons and the higher clergy, and a separate House of Commons for knights and burgesses.

In time, Parliaments would depose one king and enthrone another, formally require royal "redress of grievances" before voting money, and stipulate that only the new House of Commons could originate money bills. But several centuries were to pass before Parliament gained this real ascendancy. Politics was usually dominated by the king, the nobles and the clergy, who in turn used Parliament to attain their own ends. The men of "Commons" stood silent in the background, not daring to address their monarch and their betters except through an official "speaker."

THE KINGS OF ENGLAND

KINGS OF WESSEX
802-839	Egbert
839-858	Ethelwulf
858-860	Ethelbald
860-866	Ethelbert
866-871	Ethelred
871-899	Alfred

SAXON KINGS
899-924	Edward the Elder
924-940	Aethelstan
940-946	Edmund
946-955	Edred
955-959	Edwy
959-975	Edgar
975-978	Edward the Martyr
978-1016	Ethelred the Unready
1016	Edmund Ironside

DANISH KINGS
1016-1035	Canute
1035-1040	Harold
1040-1042	Harthacnut

SAXON KINGS
1042-1066	Edward the Confessor
1066	Harold, Earl Godwin

NORMAN KINGS
1066-1087	William I (the Conqueror)
1087-1100	William II
1100-1135	Henry I
1135-1154	Stephen

HOUSE OF PLANTAGENET
1154-1189	Henry II
1189-1199	Richard I (Lion-Heart)
1199-1216	John
1216-1272	Henry III
1272-1307	Edward I
1307-1327	Edward II
1327-1377	Edward III
1377-1399	Richard II

HOUSE OF LANCASTER
1399-1413	Henry IV
1413-1422	Henry V
1422-1461	Henry VI

HOUSE OF YORK
1461-1483	Edward IV
1483	Edward V
1483-1485	Richard III

HOUSE OF TUDOR
1485-1509	Henry VII
1509-1547	Henry VIII
1547-1553	Edward VI
1553-1558	Mary Tudor
1558-1603	Elizabeth I

HOUSE OF STUART
1603-1625	James I
1625-1649	Charles I
1649-1660	Commonwealth (no king)
1660-1685	Charles II
1685-1688	James II
1689-1694	William III and Mary
1694-1702	William III
1702-1714	Anne

HOUSE OF HANOVER
1714-1727	George I
1727-1760	George II
1760-1820	George III
1820-1830	George IV
1830-1837	William IV
1837-1901	Victoria

HOUSE OF SAXE-COBURG AND GOTHA
1901-1910	Edward VII

HOUSE OF WINDSOR
1910-1936	George V
1936	Edward VIII
1936-1952	George VI
1952-	Elizabeth II

A dawning concept of individual worth and freedom underlay the parliamentary struggles. But the dawn was slow, and at first the freedom sought was only for the powerful few. The Magna Carta, or Great Charter, of 1215, wrested at Runnymede from the scheming King John by rebellious barons, immediately protected only them and the Church hierarchy from royal excesses. But the Magna Carta and later documents furthered the principle that even kings must live under agreed rules of law and, as the early jurist Henry of Bracton said, "under God." From this came the broader principle that *all* who wield power must act responsibly, with the result—after centuries of strife—that freedom became the acknowledged right of the many.

A MIGHTY instrument of the growth of freedom was the common law of England, which forms the basis also of American law and justice. The common law began with the verdicts of the king's judges in itinerant courts. These were royal tribunals which, almost from the time of the Conquest, gradually imposed their supremacy upon the landed barons, who had their own courts, and upon the Church, whose "ecclesiastical courts" claimed jurisdiction over what we would consider lay matters and held themselves responsible only to their bishops and to the Pope in Rome.

Off and on over the centuries, in a contest that dated almost from the time Christian missionaries had first come to the British Isles in the Sixth Century, Roman Popes and English monarchs, Catholic and non-Catholic, were involved in what *The Catholic Encyclopedia* dispassionately calls "a contest between the regal and the papal power." Because it involved nothing less than the fundamental nature of England itself, the struggle touched every phase of the country's development. For England, as for every state within Rome's reach, the issue at bottom was whether the country should develop as a regional subdivision of papal Christendom or as a separate and independent nation. Even before Martin Luther in 1517 launched the Protestant Reformation, something in England's

island self impelled it to assert its own separate nationhood and thus brought many of its rulers into conflict with papal Rome.

The struggle between popes and kings was an element in the intermittent wars between England and France, where the Church was an arm of the state. From the universities of Oxford and Cambridge (founded in the 12th and 13th Centuries), where all students were required to become clergymen of lower rank, came England's first dissenters. They were "Anglican" Catholics who in the beginning were opposed not to Catholicism as such but only to papal supremacy in their land and worship. As the heretical notion that each man might be the keeper of his own soul began to spread, non-Catholic dissent developed into the Puritan spirit and movement. And soon men's insistence that their particular faith was the only true one led to such barbarous excesses as hanging, decapitating and burning those who differed from the dominant doctrine of the time.

I N this formative period the wool trade, founded on the sheep farms and cottage looms of rural England, became the country's first big business and created much new wealth. Merchants and financiers of a new middle class bought land—the indispensable prerequisite to social standing—and moved into the rising class of country gentry. Rural serfs were beginning to achieve their emancipation under a new order, and with the rise of a money economy in the 13th Century came the growth of hired labor— at cruelly low wages, but free from the personal degradations that marked servile status.

National pride also flourished, stimulated by the otherwise absurd and damaging "Hundred Years' War" of aggression against France (1337–1453). Long smothered under French and Latin, an English language enriched by both returned to general use—"so that now," wrote a chronicler in 1385, " . . . in alle the gramere scoles of Engelond, children leveth Frensche and construeth and lerneth in Englische." The freshened language burst into flower in the poems and tales of Geoffrey Chaucer (1340–1400). English translations of the Bible gave the common people their first reading matter and powerfully enlarged their horizons.

It was a rich and burgeoning England that awaited Henry VIII (1509–1547). That popular, talented and murderous monarch of many wives brought to a climax (but did not end) the long conflict with the papacy when he persuaded Parliament to break with Rome and make him "the Supreme Head" of an independent Church of England. Henry's immediate reason for doing this was that Pope Clement VII had refused to sanction his divorce from the Spanish Catherine of Aragon, his first wife and the widow of his older brother, so that he could marry his English mistress, Anne Boleyn, and produce an heir. But the royal lust was incidental to some larger considerations. Among other things, acceptance of the Pope's refusal to annul the marriage to the Catholic Catherine would have signified not only submission to the will of Rome but through this, a demeaning subjection to the powerful influence of Catherine's nephew, the King of Spain. Although his motives were mixed and many of the consequences were tragic, Henry's break with Rome was a necessary declaration of national independence.

Under Queen Elizabeth (1558–1603), who was the third of Henry's children to follow him on the throne and the inaugurator of the second period of British history, the England that Henry had loosed was able to send its ships, freebooters, explorers and colonists forth into a world then dominated by Spain and France. At home—with the help of Sir Francis Drake and some providential storms—it defeated an Armada sent against it by Spain in 1588.

APART from the resourceful and dauntless Queen, four men personify the mystery, horror and glory of that awakening age. First there was John Stubbs, a prominent lawyer and religious enthusiast who had presumed to advise "the Virgin Queen" not to marry a Frenchman, and thereby lost his right hand on the scaffold at her order. He waved aloft his stump and cried, "Long live the Queen!"

Then there was Sir Walter Raleigh. A gallant adventurer who conceived the idea of colonizing Virginia and otherwise served his Queen well, he was tried for treason under her successor, James I, and sentenced to die as follows: ". . . you shall be drawn upon a hurdle [a kind of sledge] through the open streets to the place of execution, there to be hanged and cut down alive, and your body shall be opened, your heart and bowels plucked out, and your privy members cut off and thrown into the fire before your eyes. Then your head to be stricken off from your body, and your body shall be divided into four quarters, to be disposed of at the King's pleasure." In the end, after a reprieve and rearrest, Raleigh was merely beheaded.

THIS same King James was something of a scholar and amateur writer who maintained that he ruled by divine right. He consented to the translation of the Bible that bears his name, thereby giving England and the world a work of transcendent beauty.

Finally there was "the divine Shakespeare." How was his lyric genius (and that of others almost his equal) able to flourish amid the cruelties of the time of Elizabeth and James? The historian Trevelyan provides one answer: "Shakespeare and his friends, standing as they did outside the dangerous world of religious and political controversy, enjoyed in their own spacious domains a freedom of spirit perhaps irrecoverable."

The English spirit had its ups and downs. In 1649, at the height of the incessant struggle between Parliament and the Crown, Englishmen shocked themselves by beheading King Charles I and abolishing the monarchy for 11 years. Under the able Oliver Cromwell and his Puritan Roundheads (so called because they cut their hair short), the English then learned things about themselves that they never forgot.

One lesson was that a republican type of government, in this case called the Commonwealth, did not suit England. When Cromwell changed the government and ruled alone as Protector, the country learned that personal dictatorships would not work either: Cromwell's written constitutions and rather rigid approach to government proved alien to the English character. Cromwell himself eventually concluded that England needed a king, although he declined to accept the crown when it was offered to him. He died in 1658, and two years later a chastened Parliament called to the restored throne the beheaded King's exiled son, Charles II.

During his reign, which is known as "the Restoration," the English outdid themselves with contradictions. The same Englishmen who delighted in the bawdy cynicism of Restoration drama gloried in the godly grandeur of John Milton's epic poem, *Paradise Lost.* They barred Roman Catholics from public office, confining that privilege to communicants of the established Anglican Church, and jailed the Baptist tinker John Bunyan, who disagreed with *both* Roman Catholics and Anglicans. During 12 years in prison he wrote his great prose allegory, *Pilgrim's Progress.* Although it was a time of intense national pride, the profligate King Charles and his government subsisted for years on huge bribes from the King of France, who hoped thereby to strengthen the cause of Roman Catholicism in England.

THE last of England's Catholic monarchs, Charles's brother James II, tried and failed to accomplish the same thing. The reaction to his attempt brought on the "Glorious Revolution," a series of events beginning in 1688 that culminated in the crowning of William and Mary in 1689 and completed the political foundations of modern England. Parliament permanently established its ascendancy over the Crown and provided by written law that only Protestants could be kings and queens of England. A historic "Bill of Rights" restated and confirmed the citizen's right to petition his government, provided guarantees against excessive bail or fines, and deprived the king of his power to suspend or dispense with laws. These and similar principles were as yet incompletely applied, but they represented enormous steps toward general liberty and justice. In 1707, during the reign of Queen Anne, "Great Britain" came into formal existence when Scotland combined with England and Wales in an Act of Union, thereby at last bringing the whole island under one government.

Meanwhile England's influence was expanding overseas. Indeed, the country possessed the beginnings of an empire before this could rightly be called "the British Empire." England acquired its first colony, Newfoundland, in 1583. By the time of the Glorious Revolution, the royally chartered East India Company and others had set a pattern of mercantile conquest, first for profit and only second for political power, that was to prevail for three centuries. Company armies, armed merchant ships, "privateers" who were really licensed pirates, and finally slave hunters and sellers—all competed against Spanish, Portuguese, French and Dutch rivals for gain and territory in India, southeastern Asia, the American West Indies and Africa. The Royal Navy, regular British land forces and duly constituted British administrators usually finished and consolidated the private conquests.

The 13 American colonies, founded partly by private adventurers and partly by settlers such as the Pilgrim Fathers seeking religious freedom, formed the core of "the first empire," and it is said to have ended when they won their independence. But in Canada, the West Indies, India and Africa, the British retained the makings of their second empire—the one that we now refer to as the British Empire—and it was rapidly expanded and consolidated in the 19th Century.

DURING the 18th Century the island nation grew in numbers (from seven million in 1700 to 14 million in the early 1800s) and in many other ways. The savage persecution of religious dissenters largely ceased and Englishmen generally became kinder (though hardly kind) to each other. It was a time of many-talented Englishmen: the essayists Joseph Addison and Richard Steele, for example, were members of Parliament; the novelist Henry Fielding was also a magistrate who did much to suppress crime and to establish an effective police. Such other literary immortals as Daniel Defoe, Jonathan Swift and Samuel Johnson influenced and enriched the political controversies and literary developments of their day.

Adam Smith, the Scottish economist who wrote *The Wealth of Nations* advising governments to let business alone, had a permanent influence on his own and later times. Sir Robert Walpole, the first prime minister on the modern model, developed and strengthened the Cabinet system that is still the heart of British administration. Walpole and his father-and-son successors, the two William Pitts, distributed sinecures, pensions and bribes and corrupted public processes on a scale that would be incredible today. But they and their contemporaries prepared the way for the spectacular rise of England and the British Empire in Queen Victoria's era, which formed a large part of the third great period of British history.

THIS was the time of Lord Nelson, the admiral who lived openly with his mistress, Lady Hamilton, and died triumphant at the Battle of Trafalgar. It was the time of the "Iron" Duke of Wellington, the doughty soldier (and later prime minister) who viewed the populace with contempt and brought down the French Emperor Napoleon at the Battle of Waterloo.

A gentler but no less formidable prime minister, Lord Melbourne, taught the young Queen Victoria the arts of government and so enabled her to keep a strong hand on public policy, even though monarchs by then merely reigned and no longer really ruled. Benjamin Disraeli, the extraordinary "Dizzy," delighted the little Queen by having her titled "Empress of India" during one of his turns as prime minister. Like many other Englishmen, Disraeli had viewed the growing British Empire as a nuisance and complained about "these wretched colonies." But he came to be a mighty advocate and builder of the Empire and, among other acts for its benefit, bought control of the Suez Canal from the ruler of Egypt. Under Disraeli and other prime ministers of the time (notably William Gladstone), Canada and Australia became partially autonomous entities within the Empire and thereby foreshadowed the Commonwealth of today.

Elemental decency was at last introduced into British politics during the 19th and early 20th Centuries. Wholesale and open bribery went out of fashion as an accepted device of government. After a series of reforms of the House of Commons, a decisive proportion of parliamentary seats was no longer filled from "rotten boroughs"—phony constituencies controlled by titled aristocrats. The electorate, which totaled less than 450,000 in the early 1800s, was progressively broadened until it included practically all adult Britons except women (they won the vote in 1918). The Church of England's indirect domination of Parliament and of higher education ended when non-Anglicans were by stages permitted to vote, to hold public office and to attend Oxford and Cambridge Universities. Universal, government-supported elementary education was also adopted, along with other social measures which led in time to today's welfare state.

THE Britain that mourned Victoria's death in 1901, however, was still a place of immense disparities in well-being. While a few great landed aristocrats had virtually tax-free incomes of close to five thousand dollars *a day*, the working masses did well to earn five dollars a week. In the final years of British world ascendancy, when the country's continuing status as a great power was taken for granted, further social and political reforms were brought about in the kind of quiet, gradual revolution for which Britons are famous.

A participant in the parliamentary battles that accompanied these reforms was the brash young Winston Churchill. Some 40 years later, during the second of two exhausting world wars, he was to growl that he did not propose to preside over the liquidation of the British Empire. But he lived to observe that liquidation in process —and to personify the enduring Britain that survives it.

BARBARIC SAXONS clutching crude weapons swim and wade ashore in an early invasion of England. Liking the climate, they returned to clear the forests and to farm.

CIVILIZED SAXON, King Alfred (*below*) visits a monastery school. The epitome of Anglo-Saxon culture, Alfred was an educated ruler who codified the country's laws.

A Culture Born of Barbarism

The civilization of modern Britain germinated among pagan barbarians from northern Europe who originally brought to the British Isles little more than spears and some primitive farming implements.

The Angles, the Saxons and the Jutes were too remote to have been much affected by Roman culture when they first began crossing the North Sea in the Fourth Century from their rude homes in the lower Rhine Valley, in Denmark and along the Dutch coast. They came originally as fast-striking despoilers, but returned eventually as settlers. At the end of the Sixth Century, missionaries planted the seeds of Roman Christianity, and throughout the next several centuries the monks taught people better ways of farming, opened schools, brought books from Europe and established the traditions of scholarship which persist today.

From early customs, which were reinforced by the decisions of later tribunals, emerged the precepts that lie at the core of American as well as of British justice. Later events would bring vast changes to English life, but would never entirely erase the strong Anglo-Saxon characteristics formed more than a thousand years ago.

WISE MONARCH, King Canute, who took power in 1017, shows that despite his command the tide does not halt. Unlike some later monarchs, he knew royalty's limits.

CONTENTION *between kings and subjects established the rights of each*

CORNERED RULER, King John bowed to his rebellious barons at Runnymede in 1215 and agreed to sign the Magna Carta, which curbed the absolute power of the British throne.

CRUCIAL DOCUMENT, the Magna Carta (*detail, left*) guaranteed certain rights and freedoms to both the nobility and the people. It is the basis of Britain's constitutional law.

CRITICAL BATTLE was fought in 1265 in the beautiful Vale of Evesham (*opposite*). A royal victory over a powerful rebel baron, Simon de Montfort, restored the king to power.

TUDOR TIMES gave England great men, greater institutions and an enduring architecture. Arrogant Henry VIII (*left*), though he led a boisterous life, helped build his country by developing the navy and founding the Church of England. He kept his children at an immense mansion, Hatfield (*right*).

TRIUMPH AT TRAFALGAR by Britain's Lord Nelson on October 21, 1805 (*above*), crushed Napoleon's last hope of naval hegemony and confirmed Britannia's dominance of the seas. In this painting of the battle, two British columns of ships (*center and right background*) slice into the French-Spanish fleet (*right foreground to left background*).

VICTORY AT WATERLOO by the Duke of Wellington on June 18, 1815 (*below*), sent Napoleon back into exile and ended the 20-year-long Anglo-French conflict. In Felix Philippoteaux's painting, a square of Scottish Highland soldiers (*left foreground*) and other British troops on the hill behind them turn back a fierce French cavalry charge.

MEN OF GREATNESS *led England in the early modern era. One reshaped the government, another the nation's idea of duty*

A GREAT YOUNG MAN, William Pitt (*opposite*, *far left*), addresses Commons. He became prime minister at 24 in 1783, endowing the post with unprecedented power.

A GRAND OLD MAN, William Gladstone (*below*), is shown in a portrait by Richmond. Prime minister four times, ending in 1894, he set a righteous example for the Empire.

MONARCH ON TOUR of a diminishing realm, Elizabeth smilingly accepts a little Nigerian's flowers. A colony at the time of the visit in 1956, Nigeria now governs itself.

3

A Painful Decline in Power

IN the centuries between the middle 1500s and our time—the second and third historical periods as described in Chapter 2—Britain developed from a minor island country into the world's most powerful nation. It became the master of an empire that embraced one fourth of the earth's people and land areas. At the peak of its ascendancy, imperial Britain was the leader and policeman of its world, and its grandeur and power lasted well into the present century.

Then, in the space of a few years following World War II—during the fourth historical period—most of the power melted away. Partly through its own doing and partly as the result of vast changes in the world, Britain became what many of its citizens took a morbid pleasure in calling "Little England"—or, in a later revision of that demeaning phrase, "Little Britain."

This "Little Britain" was in some respects a sick Britain. Serious commentators wrote of "the suspicion, envy and prejudice that drive a less than great power into recurrent, if half-hearted, xenophobia," and of "a frightful paralysis of the will" caused in part by "the psychological difficulty of adapting from great-power to second-rate international status." An eminent Briton spoke of "a country with a gag in its mouth and ropes around its wrists" and another of a tendency to escape from frustration in "hating everybody at the same time—the Americans, the Europeans, the Russians, the Chinese, and even some of the emergent states."

A notion that Britain could escape the world conflict with Communist power by withdrawing from such alliances as NATO, and thereby attain a new form of political and moral leadership, appealed to many Britons throughout the 1950s and for a time was near to being the doctrine of the Labour party. That illusion finally waned, although traces of it survived. In the early 1960s the Labour party proposed to abandon the "costly pretense" that Britain could afford to maintain its own arsenal of nuclear weapons. But its purpose was to bring Britain's commitments into scale with its resources, rather than to repudiate them.

NOTHING went quite right for Britain in the early 1960s. For the first time in its history, general well-being rather than general poverty was the lot of most of its people. But a sagging economy and creeping unemployment shook confidence in the widened prosperity just when it seemed to be both generating and reflecting a resurgence of national vigor. The Conservative prime minister, Harold Macmillan, had brought his country near to economic union with Europe's Common Market, at the cost of weakening the already feeble British Commonwealth, when President de Gaulle of France brutally blocked the British entry. The Labour party's new leader, Harold Wilson, described in the House of Commons the "intolerable humiliation" that De Gaulle's action heaped upon Britain and its people—"naked and shivering in the cold outside," said Wilson, "while others decide our fate."

Most of the changes that brought this baffled and beset Little Britain into being date from World War I. When that holocaust began in 1914, the Royal Navy ruled the waves from the English Channel to the far Pacific. British satraps represented not only the majesty but the real might of the Crown from Ottawa to Singapore. British bankers and merchants pervaded the world's commerce. Britain's colonial administrators, judges, soldiers and policemen maintained order and British power in great areas of Africa and Asia and on islands in every ocean. Britain's world position seemed impregnable. Its early decline, in fact, was so slow as to be almost imperceptible.

AT first the changes were largely in relative strength. Although Britain had suffered frightful losses of men and treasure in World War I, its empire was still intact, and its great-power status was not seriously challenged for many years afterward. The telling change in those years was that Britain was displaced as the world's number one power by the United States. The import of this change was somewhat obscured during the two decades of 1920–1940, when the U.S. was slow to recognize the implications and responsibilities of its new power.

During and after World War II, however, the decline of Britain in both relative and absolute power became apparent. There was no doubting that the incomparable steadfastness of the British people during the first two years of that war had made the ultimate victory possible. But, as Sir Winston Churchill himself acknowledged, Britain could not have "stood alone" during that period without the material help of the United States. This fact is hardly to the credit of the Americans, who let the British and others do the fighting for them until Japan's attack on Pearl Harbor forced them into all-out war. But it must be taken into account in any assessment of British power then and later. The struggle at once exhausted Britain and showed while the war was being won that the foundations of British hegemony had already been eroded.

In victory's bitter aftermath, Britain found

itself in a world where there were only two really "great" powers, the United States and the Soviet Union. And, apart from the rise of these other world powers, there was a visible and appalling loss of strength and resiliency on the part of Britain itself. Only rigid austerity in the daily lives of its people, together with a $3.75 billion credit and a $622 million cash loan from the U.S., enabled Britain to get through the years just after 1945. A devastating, island-wide blizzard in early 1947, which all but brought the country to its knees economically, had a profound psychological effect on a populace still weary from the war years. The government's difficulties and delays in making up coal and power shortages and in repairing flood damage created a sense of acute depression and irritation on the part of average Britons that was at least as agonizing as the actual physical discomfort.

A brave attempt in the same year to free current international dealings in the British pound from wartime controls, and thus demonstrate that Britain at the core was as sound as ever, ended in an alarming display of monetary weakness and the panicky restoration of controls. When the same controls were relaxed a few years later, Britain was in better shape—partly because it had in the meantime devalued the pound— and did very well without them.

IN the end, however, it was the rapid dissolution of the British Empire that shook Britons most profoundly. The full effect of this development was delayed for several years, but the shock was all the greater when it finally hit home. It is difficult to remember now that the British Empire was almost as extensive in 1947 as it had ever been. True, the growth of a Commonwealth of self-ruling Dominions within the Empire, starting with Canada in 1867, had diluted British power. But both the Dominions and the wide variety of colonies and dependent territories in the Empire proper still owed allegiance to the British Crown and looked to Britain for leadership.

At this time, millions of homeside Britons variously took the Empire for granted, regarded it as rather a nuisance or felt somewhat ashamed of it. But, whatever their feelings about it, the vast majority took comfort from their knowledge that the sun never set on the British flag. It was still possible for a beefy Canadian general, who like many "colonials" was more British than the British, to turn purple when an American mentioned the newfangled Commonwealth, and to roar: "God damn it, sir, never say Commonwealth to me—say EMPAH!"

THE last years of "empah" were 1947–1948, when Britain granted full freedom and self-determination to India, Pakistan (newly seceded from India), Ceylon and Burma. These were free to go it alone or to join the "British Commonwealth of Nations," which had replaced the previous "Commonwealth and Empire." Only Burma stayed out of the new Commonwealth. Ceylon came in as an independent Dominion, nominally under the British Crown but actually on its own in every substantial respect. India and Pakistan accepted Dominion status and then became Republics; they remained within the Commonwealth, but they no longer paid allegiance to the Crown and were tied to Britain only by common interest and voluntary association. During this period the word "Emperor" or "Empress" was dropped from the title of British monarchs and the phrase "British Empire" vanished from official use.

As recently as 1960, an official description of the new Commonwealth still said that it "covers a quarter of the entire land surface of the earth," and that "within it live more than a quarter of all the people in the world." But today's Commonwealth of more than 723 million people in 80 sovereign states, colonies and other dependent territories is a very different thing from the 1947 Commonwealth and Empire. Apart from Britain's own 53 million people in its island homeland, 35 million of the new Commonwealth's population are ruled directly by London, but this number is bound to diminish as old colonies progress through successive stages of internal self-government toward full nationhood. Among the countries that in recent years

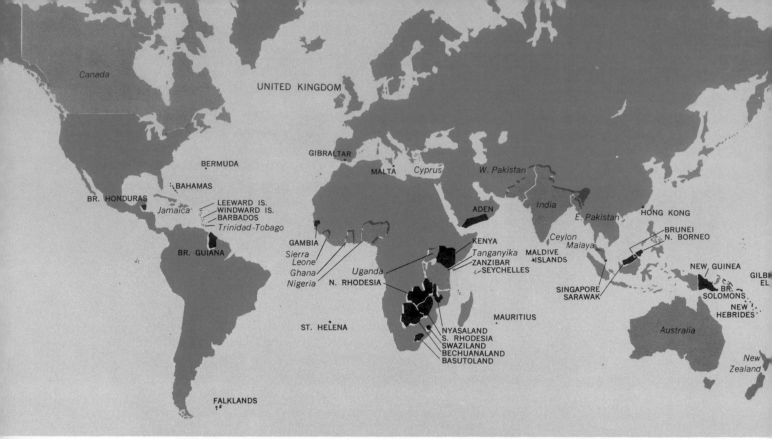

THE TRANSFORMED EMPIRE is still far flung, but only bits and pieces are now governed from London. Areas shown in light gray (*with their names in italics*) are independent countries linked to the Commonwealth under various arrangements. Areas in solid black (*bold type*) are colonies, territories and other dependencies.

completed this transition are Jamaica and Trinidad and Tobago in the West Indies and Tanganyika and Uganda in Africa. All became sovereign states within the Commonwealth.

The Commonwealth's independent members make their own policies and choose their own political courses. They disagree among themselves and with Britain far more often than they agree. At the United Nations, for example, a single "Commonwealth position" is unknown, and the British representatives have cause to be pleasantly surprised when such Commonwealth members as India and Ghana side with their former master.

This remarkably loose association is something of a puzzle even to its own members. India's Prime Minister Jawaharlal Nehru described the Commonwealth in 1950 as a "rather strange and odd collection of nations" which "has found some kind of invisible link by seeing that practically there is no link." The late Prime Minister Peter Fraser of New Zealand remarked that the Commonwealth association in essence is "independence with something

added, and not independence with something taken away." With their characteristic delight in institutional obfuscation, the British clung for years to the hope that the mystic bonds of the new Commonwealth would somehow underpin and enhance British power and prestige almost—if not altogether—as well as the old Commonwealth and Empire had.

This hope proved to be sound only in the economic field, and not entirely so even there. All British dependencies and all of the Commonwealth countries except Canada belong to "the sterling area," an economic entity which is almost as esoteric as the Commonwealth. The sterling-area members also include such non-Commonwealth countries as Burma, Iceland, Jordan, Libya, the Irish Republic and the British-protected states of the Persian Gulf, and their common characteristic is that they finance the bulk of their foreign trade in British pounds sterling, paying for their imports and taking payments for their exports in that currency. They also maintain a fixed relationship between the value of their own currencies (Indian rupees,

Burmese kyats, etc.) and that of the British pound. Most of them do their foreign banking in London, buy and sell gold on the London market and even keep their currency reserves there, usually in the Bank of England.

The general effect of all this is to maintain a huge pool of liquid working capital, with which almost half of the world's trade is financed. More to the point for Britain, the day-to-day management of that pool is centered in London. The proportion of Britain's own trade conducted with the sterling area is higher now than it was in 1938, and the sterling system remains a mark of British prestige.

BUT Britain's traditional economic ties with the sterling area and the Commonwealth entail liabilities as well as assets. For a variety of reasons, it is difficult for Britain to trade on equal terms with both the Commonwealth and continental Europe. How to retain its Commonwealth trade and at the same time keep and expand vital markets on the continent is one of postwar Britain's most troublesome problems.

The historic assumption has been that the continental countries value Britain's business, friendship and support sufficiently to welcome the country's participation in continental arrangements, however limited and grudging that participation may be. Now this assumption is dead. Germany, Italy, Belgium and the other two continental members resented General de Gaulle's assertion of French mastery over the Common Market and showed some sympathy for excluded Britain. But they, along with France, had long since made it painfully clear to Britain that they could get along without its participation and trade if they had to. A rival economic grouping organized by Britain and known informally as the "Outer Seven" had neither succeeded in itself nor materially strengthened the British position. These setbacks, coupled with the realization that the diluted Commonwealth contributed very little to effective British power, created something close to a state of schizophrenia in the collective mind of Little Britain.

It might have been supposed that the years of strict rationing, scarce goods and generally grimy austerity just after the war underlay such psychological strains, and that the predicament would vanish with the coming of prosperity. But this was not the case. In the 1950s Britain's domestic economy, stimulated by its own partial recovery, by the pound's devaluation and by improved trading conditions abroad, went into a boom that began to slacken only in the early 1960s. The rationing of personal goods ended in 1954 and the boom was in joyous swing when, in 1956, the abortive attempt of Britain, France and Israel to reoccupy the Suez Canal Zone militarily brought postwar Britain's frustrations and inward ills boiling to the surface. Although all three nations collaborated in the attack on Egypt, Prime Minister Sir Anthony Eden was the prime mover and controlling figure in much of the affair.

Analyzing this fantastic episode, Professor H. C. Allen of the University of London said that the attack and the reaction to it were due in part to the strains of the "huge process of political disengagement" involved in the dissolution of the Empire, and to "the emotional sensibilities of Britons about their declining influence and prestige in international affairs." When the Egyptian revolutionaries who had deposed King Farouk seized the Suez Canal from its mainly British and French owners, "a long-sensitive nerve, that of declining imperial greatness, lay exposed and was touched upon the raw by this threat to the canal, which still loomed so large in the inner recesses of most British minds as the 'lifeline' of Empire."

IF the attempt to retake Suez by force was a "violent, astounding storm" in reaction to the country's accumulated "psychological tension," as Professor Allen and other Britons say it was, its abject failure—when Eden had to call the whole thing off largely because of world-wide protests—both created and revealed additional tensions. Many Britons felt that President Eisenhower's private, irritated protests to Eden were responsible more than anything else for compelling the prime minister to abandon the Suez operation. A wave of sheer, cold hatred for the United States thereupon swept London and was even shared by Britons who personally deplored Eden's adventure. Several weeks after the event, old British friends of an American visitor hesitated to invite him to their clubs because his presence there might provoke unseemly outbursts. London hotel clerks, taxi drivers and airport attendants treated Americans with chill, minimal courtesy. A British Cabinet minister lapsed into unprintable invective in alleging that the U.S. had deliberately left Britain "up the creek" at Suez.

But the most severe shock at the time was confined to a very small number of British officials and politicians who understood that neither Eisenhower's protests nor Russia's violent threats to intervene on the side of Egypt were the most important factors in the abandonment of the attempt. These played their part, but a clinching factor was the threat made at the time by India and Ceylon, with Canada only a little less insistent, to leave the Commonwealth, thereby disrupting it beyond repair, if Eden did not immediately halt the Suez invasion.

To the Britons in high places who were aware of it, this reaction demonstrated as nothing else could have how insubstantial and elusive the Commonwealth relationship was when put to a severe test. At the crux of the Common Market negotiations, when Britain had to make its agonizing and fundamental choice between the continent and the Commonwealth, it chose the continent. Although the choice proved to be futile, the rest of the Commonwealth would not soon forget or forgive it.

TODAY, barred from immediate integration with Europe and to some extent alienated from the Commonwealth, Little Britain displays a mixed set of attitudes that are at once fascinating and disturbing to friendly observers. A deep apathy coexists with a mood of searching, often bitter and potentially fruitful re-examination. Many Britons yearn to recapture their old confidence in themselves—and

they perceive that the very wish to do so indicates that something rare and strong has been misplaced if not irretrievably lost. As the virulent, damn-the-bomb neutralism of the 1950s appears to subside, a kind of national wariness emerges. There is a time of pause, of *waiting* for solutions. A strong new pull toward affiliation with continental Europe, thwarted for the moment but by no means destroyed, still coincides with plain isolationism of a kind quite similar to the isolationism that dominated American attitudes for many years. But the peculiar nationalism of those Britons who argue that Little Britain should deliberately make itself still smaller is losing its appeal in a period when British power shrinks beyond the point that even they had desired.

DEEP dislike and envy of the United States in world affairs are manifested by Britons along with the warmest assurances of personal and official friendship. While some Britishers demand an immediate and total break with United States policy, others quiver with delight at the slightest indication that their prime minister stands high in the regard of Washington officialdom. Britons depressed by their country's decline in world status take an almost desperate pride in such domestic achievements as their welfare services and the vigorous replanning and dispersion of their overcrowded industrial centers. "It gives us a chance," says a Scottish planning official, "to prove that we can still do something worthwhile." Conversely, frustration is compounded when the best of such efforts prove insufficient for the country's overwhelming needs.

Although their country is changing and their attitudes toward the outside world fluctuate rapidly, "the British people," as Harold Macmillan has said, "do not change." Little Britain has plenty of ills and defects, but in its healthier aspects it seems to suit its citizens very well. And why not? For most of them, it has brought a far higher standard of living and well-being than they ever knew in Britain's day of power and imperial glory.

The setting sun of a great empire slants across the Egyptian desert in 1954 as a British aircraftsman walks a final patrol at Suez.

The Surge and Ebb of Empire

In less than three centuries, Britain elevated itself from a tiny island state into history's greatest power, and patriots boasted, "The sun never sets on the British Empire." But, unlike any of its predecessors, it devised its own dissolution, transforming Empire into Commonwealth and bestowing self-rule everywhere. Now Britain is training its last colonies to go their own way.

MILITARY GENIUS of Robert Clive won India for Britain. Here, atop a local potentate's hunting lodge, Clive surveys enemy lines in the 1757 Battle of Plassey. But for him, most of India might have become French territory.

COLONIAL FEALTY is proclaimed by the people of Aden (*below*), greeting the Prince of Wales in 1921. The royal visitor, who is now the Duke of Windsor, later recalled the contrast between this and riots he met while in India.

TELL DADDY WE ARE ALL HAPPY UNDER BRITISH RULE

IMPERIAL PRIDE was at its height in 1851 when Queen Victoria, the Garter's blue sash adorning her pink gown, opened a great industrial exhibition in the Crystal Palace. To her, to the crimson-coated Prince Albert and the kilted Prince of Wales beside her, and to the guests from afar, it seemed the power behind the pomp would last forever.

GIVING UP POWER, the Empire schooled former colonies such as Ghana in democratic ways and then granted them independence. Ghana gained Dominion status in 1957. Here its National Assembly—patterned after Britain's Parliament—opens with the British governor general as chief of state on the gold throne. When Ghana became a republic in 1960, Kwame Nkrumah (*fourth from right in first row at left*) became the state's chief executive.

BEWIGGED JUDGE, Sir Arku Korsah (*opposite*) wears a crimson robe as Chief Justice. He studied law in England and was once a member of Ghana's Legislative Council.

HARDY YOUTHS from Commonwealth countries receive physical training at a Devon school. Such young people, Britain knows, will decide the Commonwealth's future.

At a critical moment in British politics following the resignation of Anthony Eden early in 1957, Harold Macmillan leaves Buckingham

Palace, having just been designated prime minister by the Queen.

4

An Oddly Efficient Government

THE great institutions that frame and implement the public life of Britain are ornamental, illogical and so encumbered by the past that they seem to be buried in it. In short, they are very British. Yet, despite all their antique pageantry and ceremony, they work well. The British, who are proud of their reputation as a nation of muddlers, tend to be disconcerted when confronted with evidence that they have one of the world's most efficient governments.

Everything in the public structure begins with and rests upon that elusive oddity, the British Constitution. The best-known fact about the Constitution is that it is unwritten. Yet this "fact" is not quite true, for some parts of the Constitution do exist in writing: the Magna Carta, certain laws enacted by Parliament and various portions of the common law declared by judges are examples. Even these parts of it have never been condensed and codified in a single document. But if they had, the Constitution still would not be wholly written. Some of its most important provisos consist of unwritten "conventions": customs, accepted beliefs and common attitudes that have accumulated over the centuries. These have the effect of constitutional law, even though there would be nothing on paper for a court to enforce if they were violated. Among them are the principle that the monarch reigns but does not rule, the precious guarantee of free speech and a wide range of other protections for Britain's prized "liberty of the subject."

Sir Ivor Jennings, a contemporary constitutional authority, touched on the most baffling aspect of the Constitution when he observed that it "consists of institutions and not of the paper that describes them." Thus the monarchy, Parliament, the Cabinet, the major political parties and the courts of law are actually parts of the very Constitution that defines and restrains them. When they change in composition or practice, the Constitution changes with them. Yet, as a result of the most powerful and least definable fact of British public life, they change only in ways and within limits that the Constitution permits.

ANY change that might exceed or violate these limits, which are more often understood than specified, is literally unthinkable to the British people. If such a change did occur and were not quickly corrected, the electorate would have an early opportunity to throw out the political party in power and compel correction. In the last (and unlikely) extremity the British public would have a constitutional right to rebel. Or so the British people have come to assume. It is upon this broad assumption—in itself a part of the Constitution—that British government is founded and works.

In this sense the British Constitution may be described as a cumulative agreement between the governed and the governors. Those who are governed agree that they will submit to responsible government; for their part, the governors agree that they will govern responsibly.

At the apex of the constitutional system is the monarch, now Queen Elizabeth II. The Queen's

position and role dramatically illustrate both the system's contradictions and its strengths. She is all but powerless, yet the powers of the government are *her* powers, diffused by long evolution among *her* Parliament, *her* prime minister, *her* Cabinet, *her* courts. Parliament, where the greatest concentration of public power now lies, is still in its corporate whole "the Queen in Parliament" (or the King, when a king reigns). The Cabinet, where the powers of administration are concentrated, is still "the Queen in Council." Such phrases are not mere symbolic anachronisms: the Queen is not there, but her power is, and in an unfathomable British way the power seems particularly real because, although it is wielded by others, it remains the power of a single person, the monarch.

WALTER BAGEHOT, a 19th Century student of the Constitution, said that three rights remain to the modern British sovereign: "the right to be consulted, the right to encourage, the right to warn." These rights are exercised largely with and through the sovereign's prime minister, to an extent that depends upon the personal relationship between him and the monarch. Occasionally, however, a vestige of direct power is returned to the sovereign. Such an occasion befell the young Queen Elizabeth in 1957 when Sir Anthony Eden, ill and discredited by the failure of his attempt to seize Suez, resigned as prime minister. The Queen, who usually has a choice only in principle, had to choose between two rivals for the succession, Harold Macmillan and R. A. Butler. In keeping with the constitutional requirement that the sovereign act only upon the advice of others, Queen Elizabeth sought the counsel of Sir Winston Churchill and another Conservative party dignitary, the Marquess of Salisbury. They obviously guided her thinking, but in the end Harold Macmillan was *her* choice.

The powers and responsibilities held by the Queen's prime minister are enormous, but a fundamental fact of the British system is that they are not solely his. They reside not in him but in his Cabinet. In its nature and workings "the Cabinet system" is almost as elusive as the Constitution of which it is a vital part. As immutable as if it were written in stone, the principle of Cabinet responsibility is written nowhere: it is entirely a matter of convention.

In essence, the Cabinet system is a device for assuring collective rather than individual responsibility at the summit of British policy and administration. Certain ministers at the head of major departments (the Treasury, the Home Office and the Foreign Office, for example) are always members of the Cabinet. Otherwise the membership of this body is determined by the current prime minister and therefore varies in number from one government to another. Policy questions may be fiercely argued within the Cabinet, but the argument ends there.

In cases of unresolved dispute, a strong prime minister can impose his policy on the Cabinet. But it has no force until it *is* Cabinet policy, and any minister who cannot support the adopted policy resigns from the government. On the other hand, the Cabinet is wholly free to support or to dump a minister who makes a glaring mistake or for some other reason gets into trouble with Parliament or the public.

LARGE though the outward contrasts are between the British and the American governments, the most significant difference between the "unwritten" British Constitution and the written U.S. Constitution is a matter not of form but of philosophy. The British Constitution embodies the proposition that supreme authority must be concentrated at one point in government if public power is to be effectively exercised. This point of supreme authority was once the monarchy; now it is the "Queen in Parliament." The U.S. Constitution is based on the principle that supreme authority must never be placed at any single point in government if public power is to be *safely* exercised. This gives rise to the familiar American separation of powers between the executive, legislative and judicial branches. In the U.S., none of these three is supreme over the others, but in Britain the Parliament stands supreme over all other public entities, including the monarchy and the courts.

From this supremacy flows the fact—remarkable to Americans—that the British courts have no power whatever to review, modify or strike down Acts of Parliament. In theory, British judges may not even "interpret" parliamentary law in the American sense of making a statute mean what the judges think it means. Parliament, on the other hand, is free in principle to amend or strike down any part of the common law as it is declared by judges in the course of deciding particular cases. If Parliament chose tomorrow to abolish the whole system of British courts, the sitting judges would be constitutionally bound to accept the result.

YET British judges are, if anything, more independent than their American counterparts. This is partly because, as individuals with enormous prestige, they are to all effects immune from either removal or public criticism once they have been appointed (usually for life). But, in a deeper sense, it is because Parliament is traditionally and constitutionally expected to exercise its unlimited power with the greatest restraint. Always at its shoulder and in its mind, after all, is the British electorate, with its seemingly un-British but thoroughly constitutional right of revolt.

This all-powerful but severely self-restrained Parliament has two chambers, the House of Lords and the House of Commons, each with its own Gothic hall in the "Palace" of Westminster in London. In early 1963 the House of Lords consisted of 923 eligible peers. Among them were four "peers of the blood royal," members of the royal family who by modern custom never participate in the affairs of the House; the two archbishops and 24 senior bishops of the Church of England, "by law established," who are considered noblemen within the House and often appear there; nine ennobled judges called "Lords of Appeal in Ordinary"; 842 hereditary dukes, marquesses, earls, viscounts and barons, including lady peers only recently made eligible to sit; and 42 "life peers"—seven baronesses and 35 barons whose titles last only for their lifetime and cannot be passed on in the normal manner of hereditary privilege.

The House of Lords lost its last real power in 1911; now it may delay, but never completely block, legislation passed by the House of Commons. But it is not so moribund as is generally supposed. It often initiates important legislation. Since the first "life peers," most of them professional politicians, were added to its membership in 1958, its debates have earned increasing respect for their liveliness and pertinence. Its members continue to hold high political posts: in a recent British government, the Earl of Home (pronounced Hume) was Foreign Secretary, Viscount Hailsham was Minister of Science and nine other Lords were ministers or junior ministers. The Labour party at one time was pledged publicly to abolish the House of Lords, but significantly it never tried to do so after it won governmental power in 1945.

THE true possessor of parliamentary power, the House of Commons, consists of 630 elected M.P.s, or Members of Parliament. Each of them represents a constituency in England (511), Scotland (71), Wales (36) or Northern Ireland (12). Members of the House have no fixed terms, but are elected for the duration of each Parliament. Parliament as an institution never dies, but particular Parliaments live only from one national election to the next. Five years is the maximum statutory period between elections, but this has been exceeded in times of crisis such as this century's two world wars. Parliamentary elections are Britain's only national elections, and M.P.s are the only national officials for whom Britons vote.

The leader of the political party with the largest number of seats in the House of Commons—preferably but not necessarily a clear majority—normally becomes the prime minister and heads the working government until its tenure and the life of the concurrent Parliament end in one of several possible ways. A majority of M.P.s may throw out a prime minister and his government by refusing to give him a vote of confidence on any measure that involves a decisive show of trust in his leadership. Whether such a vote leads to a complete change of government depends on the circumstances, but the possibility is an important element in Parliament's power. If a really crucial vote goes against the prime minister and his government, Parliament may be dissolved and nationwide elections for a new House of Commons are thereupon called.

Parliaments may also end if the prime minister, as political leader and chief strategist of his party, chooses to bring about an election by asking the reigning monarch to dissolve the House. This happened in 1959 when Prime Minister Macmillan figured (correctly) that his Conservative party stood to gain parliamentary seats by "going to the country" then instead of in 1960, when the statutory five-year tenure would have expired.

It has been said that Parliament's three main functions are to make laws, to provide public funds, and "to criticise and control the government." The third is in many respects Parliament's most vital function, and it is fulfilled principally in the House of Commons. Ministers of the Crown are almost always members of one House or the other, and since 1902 the prime minister has been drawn from Commons. There he and his fellow ministers (unless they are Lords, in which case junior ministers represent them) must regularly confront the House, defend government proposals and actions, and answer questions from the Honourable Members, who sit on tiered benches that rise one above the other from a narrow central floor area. It is there that Britain's parliamentary system of government and its party system mesh, combining to make the constitutional system work as well as it does.

HOUSE debates, superintended under strict rules by the august Speaker in his white wig and black gown—a reminder that Parliament once was more of a law court than a legislature—usually proceed in sleepy decorum. But the high, rectangular chamber sometimes crackles with invective close to insult. Such occurred in 1949 when the tempestuous Labour party leader, the late Aneurin Bevan, called Sir Winston Churchill (to his face) "this bloated bladder of lies." On many occasions, shouts of "Nonsense!" and "Shame!" accompanied by horrendous groans and counter-groans, are hurled at inept or offensive debaters from the "back benches," where ordinary members sit above and behind the dignitaries on the floor-level "front benches."

Just under the Speaker's high dais, between the front benches, stands the low "Table of the House." By slouching deep on their backbones, the senior Ministers of the Crown and their counterparts in the Opposition can rest their feet on this table. The art of the front-bench slouch is highly prized, and those who are deficient in it are at a disadvantage. Perhaps the most entrancing spectacle in Parliament is that of a British prime minister staring between his impeccable boots at the shoe soles of the Leader of the Opposition.

BRITAIN'S political parties have a specific constitutional role and status. The entire system can function properly only if *they* function properly, a fact that is never forgotten by the M.P.s who compose the respective parties in Parliament. Individual and group rebellions against the party leaderships periodically enliven British politics and Parliament's proceedings. But in general the parties are subject to a discipline and, at critical moments, display a cohesion which would seem outrageous to Republicans and Democrats in the U.S. Congress. The result is a notable stability in a system which otherwise would have all the makings of chronic instability.

The duality of British parties as political entities and as constitutional instruments of the state is illustrated by Her Majesty's Loyal Opposition. "The Opposition" is in effect the party that stands second in strength in the House of Commons at a given time, out of power and hoping to win power at the next election. As the term implies, the party has a formal duty to criticize and oppose the government of the party in power. But it also has an equally binding duty

(not always fulfilled) to assist the government by *constructive* criticism, by the avoidance of frivolous or merely malicious attack, and on occasion by substantial cooperation between the prime minister and the formally named Leader of the Opposition. The leader, often a former prime minister who may become the next one, receives a special government salary ($8,400, as compared with an ordinary M.P.'s $4,900 a year). In some ways the relationship between him and the prime minister resembles that of minority and majority leaders in the U.S. Congress, but he is regarded—and regards himself—as a servant of the state in a sense that does not apply to his American counterparts.

An institution peculiar to British parties is the Opposition "Shadow Cabinet." Its members are M.P.s or Lords who will stand first in line for ministerial appointments if and when their party wins power. They are usually designated as the minister-to-be for foreign affairs, the Treasury, the Home Office and so on. They may turn out later on to be the minister for something else, or for nothing, but great importance is attached to these selections. The bait they represent is one of the principal means by which the Opposition leader maintains discipline among his cohorts, who at best tend to be restive and rebellious when out of power.

ALTHOUGH Britain always has several political parties, two of them usually dominate. Today these two are the Conservative and Labour parties (the Liberal party, the Conservatives' principal rival until the 1920s, went into lengthy eclipse but has recently been making a comeback). The Conservative party traces its ancestry back three centuries to the time of King Charles II, when the monarch's adherents in a complicated quarrel were dubbed Tories, from an old term for outlaws. The Conservative party has generally been what the name has come to mean, a party of those who have had a propertied interest in things-as-they-are. But it has seldom been solely that. Today it owes its prosperity in large measure to its adoption of welfare, nationalization and kindred policies, originally pioneered by the Labour party, which would seem wildly radical to conservative Americans.

The Labour party, young as British parties go, has been represented in the House of Commons only since 1906. By doctrine and by history it is a true Socialist party in the classic (and non-Communist) sense, dedicated in principle to inclusive national ownership of basic industry and to welfare measures that go far beyond those of Britain's mid-century welfare state. Its Socialist doctrine and spirit stem from two main sources: the working-class movements of the 19th Century that produced the trade unions of today, and the intellectual Socialists—among them George Bernard Shaw, the playwright, and the zealous political theorists, Sidney Webb and his wife Beatrice. Around the turn of the century these intellectuals made the Fabian Society, a group of influential Socialist thinkers, a mighty factor in British politics.

After its first and, so far, only prolonged period of power (from 1945 to 1951), the Labour party discovered that it had given the British people all of the socialism in the form of nationalized industry and state welfarism that most of them wanted for a while. The question then arose: Should the party continue in its militant way, or should it soft-pedal its historically Socialist note and appeal instead to Britain's traditional conservatism? Under the leadership of the late Hugh Gaitskell, the party minimized doctrinaire socialism. Under Gaitskell's successor, Harold Wilson, it will remain moderate although it plans to renationalize the steel industry and broaden social security.

PARTIES change and party governments rise and fall, but the British Civil Service goes on forever. Although practically all Britons now take this for granted, the Civil Service has existed in something like its present form only since 1870. Yet today it is all but synonymous with government in Britain—pervasive, powerful and indispensable.

Including all permanent government employees from dockyard workers to knighted officials, there are around one million British civil servants. But those who personify the capital-letter Civil Service and its extraordinary government role number only about 3,100. They constitute two kindred elites, the "Administrative Class" of the Home Civil Service and "Branch A" of the Foreign Service. Nowadays a horde of scientists, engineers, social planners and other specialists contest with these two elites for position and preference, but the entrenched civil servants still have the upper hand and probably will keep it.

FROM them are drawn the permanent officials who staff the upper career levels of all British ministries and departments. They are the uncrowned monarchs of Whitehall, the London area where the older ministries are concentrated. To the fluid system of parliamentary government, with its unpredictable changes of ministers and junior ministers, they give a saving competence, solidity and continuity. The British welkin regularly rings with denunciations of the upper Civil Service for its snobbish policy of recruiting new personnel mainly from the best-tie schools and universities (true, but considerably less so than it used to be); for its built-in monopoly of top career posts (true, but that is what it is for); and for its tendency toward excessive caution (true). A more substantial criticism is that entrenched civil servants, whether by intention or simply because they command the channels of official information, make prisoners of their political chiefs, imposing upon them policy judgments that in constitutional principle are the sole responsibility of the ministers themselves. This has happened and it will continue to happen.

Some civil servants have not been the soul of dependability. The treachery of Guy Burgess and Donald Maclean, the career diplomats who defected to the Soviet Union in 1951, shook the rather complacent Civil Service to its well-shod heels and led to a tightening of recruitment and security practices. But it did not shake the confidence of the British public in its civil servants as a class. They have functioned too well and for too long a time at the core of a government which is noted for its endurance.

In velvet cape and plumed hat, Sir Winston Churchill (foreground) leads a procession at Windsor as he becomes a Knight of the Garter.

A Love of Pomp and Pageant

No people cherish democracy in government more zealously than the British. And no people rival them in love of the pageantry attending royal rule, or in skill at staging it. Panoply and color distinguish and dignify virtually every ceremonial phase of temporal and spiritual life. The seemingly archaic display not only manifests the people's unity, but also strengthens it.

SCULPTURED STONE at Wells (*left*) immortalizes medieval heroes such as Roger, Bishop of Salisbury (*middle*), and, below him, King Henry I.

TIMELESS SPLENDOR of Wells Cathedral (*right*), one of the oldest and noblest holy edifices, reflects the place of the Church in the life of the nation.

MITER AND ROBES worn by Geoffrey Fisher, former Archbishop of Canterbury (*at left*), betoken the authority he held as Primate of All England.

CROWN AND THRONE of the monarch (*opposite*) symbolize the royal base of governmental power. Here, in solemnity, the Queen opens Parliament.

Resplendent in red coats and black bearskin hats, the Scots Guards turn their heads in salute at Trooping the Colour. In the exciting,

clock-precise parades of such famous military units as the Guards regiments, the pageantry-loving English take a recurring delight.

APPEALING FOR VOTES, the late Hugh Gaitskell, an intellectual leader of the Labour party, delivers a campaign speech from a sunny, poster-splashed platform in Essex.

OPENING A CAMPAIGN in an austere hall in Leeds in 1950 (*opposite*), Winston Churchill speaks on behalf of a local candidate. The Tories lost that year but won in 1951.

Grim-faced Glasgow boilermakers, who work in a shipyard, listen intently as their union's district delegate urges them to walk out.

A Flexibility of Control

Although the government guides the economy, the relationship of employers and employees is unchanged, and labor unions remain powerful.

THE powers and responsibilities of Britain's national government reach deeply into the lives of the citizens—so deeply, in fact, that Britons might well be expected to feel that they are, in Shakespeare's words, "cabined, cribbed, confined" to an intolerable extent. But the British people do not feel that way. Their proud image of themselves has been affected hardly at all by the rise of the welfare state and the resulting high degree of government responsibility for the individual and collective life of the people. The British like to believe that they invented individual freedom, and they still regard themselves as highly individual, uniquely free people. Although sophisticated Britons tend to laugh nowadays at the familiar cartoon figure of John Bull, standing massive and defiantly upright on his booted feet, he still symbolizes the nation as its people see it. Britons do *not* feel that they are pampered by their government, and they generally have no sense of being under excessive government control.

Yet their national government is extraordinarily pervasive by American standards. It owns

83

and operates (through public corporations and agencies) the country's coal mines, railways, principal airlines, radio stations, electric power lines and power plants (including 10 nuclear plants built, under construction or planned), the gas industry, part of the highway trucking industry—and the Bank of England. In line with the declared national policy that in no circumstances need anyone fall below a certain minimum standard of living, the government employs all but a few hundred of the country's doctors and dentists, owns most of the hospitals and provides medical care, old-age pensions and supplementary relief where needed for the entire population.

The national government contributes cash to the support of every child in Britain. It supervises and at least partly finances all primary and secondary schools except the "public schools" —which are really private schools—and contributes to the cost of educating about 75 per cent of all university students. It watches over the pay and other standards of all police and firemen. It subsidizes and closely controls British agriculture (which grows nearly half of the food Britain consumes, the rest being imported). The government wields a variety of direct and indirect controls over British business. In the past it has rationed food and clothing, and it can do so again. It contributes to the support of theaters, art galleries, lecture courses and many other cultural activities. It undertakes to maintain full employment, but has not been able to solve the problems of 20th Century industry.

IN short, the hand and the power of the national government in Britain are everywhere. But any summary of the government's wide participation in the common life of the British is sure to be misleading, especially to Americans, unless a few key facts and attitudes bearing upon its role are explained.

First it must be understood that the national government is to all effects the *only* government in Britain. There are no equivalents in Britain of states or provinces, and therefore no state or provincial governing bodies between the national and local levels. More than 12,000 "local authorities"—county, borough, town, district and parish councils—are important elements in the total political structure. They are locally elected and they have a sturdy sense of local identity. But in many respects they are really arms of the national government: they are subject to the national authority of Parliament, operate under the supervision of national ministries, and draw more than half of their funds from the national treasury. Scotland and Wales are administered by the national government. Outside Great Britain proper, Northern Ireland has its own Parliament for regional matters, and some regional autonomy, but the national government has overriding authority.

ANOTHER fundamental fact is that the English people, who dominate the kingdom, want and are used to strong central rule. Indeed, the English spent centuries attaining a centralized government under popular control. A system of decentralized government on the American model—even though that model is being rapidly altered by Americans in favor of more and more national action—would seem both unnatural and dangerous to the English. As for the Welsh and Scots, they profess to want genuine regional autonomy, if not separate nationhood; but they know as well as the English that they are not likely ever to get either.

Since the British trust their central government and look to it for broad national action, the scope of the responsibilities and powers assumed by that government is seldom in serious dispute. The declared intention of the Labour party to increase somewhat the scope of nationalized industry is deplored by some factions in the party and is strongly opposed by the Conservatives. But the grounds for opposition are very different from those which would be raised in the United States against an equivalent program. In the U.S. the main motive of opposition would be a fear of vesting so much direct power in the national government. In Britain there is no such fear. Britons who oppose further nationalization of industry generally do so on the ground that the move would be unnecessary, ineffective and self-defeating.

The lack of fear results in some unexpected attitudes. An executive of one of Britain's largest motor-car companies recently assured an American visitor, "British businessmen are as free to run their businesses as any in the world." This free Briton's company had just been forbidden by the government to build a new factory where it wanted it, and instead had been compelled to place the factory in a different region of the country in order to stimulate employment there. The company in return had been guaranteed government financing of the planned expansion on terms that in a few years would amount to a subsidy of many millions of dollars.

Like its competitors, this motor-car company is in effect barred by government credit regulations and other measures from fully exploiting the hungry domestic market for automobiles, and is strongly encouraged to commit a big proportion of its output to increasingly-chancy foreign markets. Yet this executive's eyes bulged with astonishment when he was asked whether he and his management associates felt that they were free to determine their own policies and run their own business. He obviously considered the question to be rather foolish and irrelevant.

A GROUP of managers in several other industries evinced a kind of amused toleration when an American visitor raised a similar question with them. In this instance, however, some of them became visibly troubled as the discussion proceeded. They had the air of men who were suddenly called upon to think about and weigh factors in their lives and their work that they hitherto had taken for granted. Upon unaccustomed scrutiny, the atmosphere of governmental regulation and supervision in which they labored did not seem quite as normal as it previously had seemed. Merely discussing the subject had stirred a sleeping dog that is seldom awakened in today's Britain.

Two reasons for the general sense of independence in a highly dependent society are of special interest to Americans. One of these reasons is that the British have demonstrated that government support of a given activity does not necessarily require detailed and continuous government control of that activity—as many Americans assume it must. In subsidizing the country's universities, for example, the government turns a large sum of money every year over to a committee of educators, who apportion the funds and set the standards governing their use. The government basically determines what these standards must be, but thanks to the buffer committee the university authorities do not feel that they are under oppressive official control.

In somewhat similar fashion, the British Medical Association stands between the medical profession and the ministry that actually controls the National Health Service. This arrangement gives individual doctors a sense that they have a substantial say in their own affairs, even though these same doctors are largely paid by the national government.

THE other reason is more a matter of method than of organization: much of the public control is negative and persuasive, rather than positive and commanding. Thus no government official told the previously mentioned car-making company in so many words that it had to put its new factory where the government wanted it put. Instead, the national ministry concerned simply invoked a regulation requiring a government license for the construction of any industrial facility that occupies more than 5,000 square feet of floor space. When the necessary license had been denied for several proposed locations, the company management realized that the ministry must have a definite preference. Discreet inquiries established that this was indeed the case, and the company thereupon decided to go where it could get its license. Negotiations for the indirect but handsome subsidy then proceeded happily and everybody was content.

Neither the government officials nor the company managers concerned in this typical affair were so rude as to mention to each other that much larger considerations than the location of one factory were involved. The fact is that the government, meaning in practice the ministry officials dealing with such a matter, have the power to make things extremely uncomfortable for any British industry. For instance, the size of the purchase tax on motor cars—an added percentage of the retail price—has much to do with the volume of home sales. Parliament must approve changes in this tax, but the tax is raised or lowered only on the recommendation of the government in power, and the senior officials of interested ministries usually determine what change is recommended. When the Macmillan government reduced the tax from 50 per cent to 25 per cent of the list price in 1962, the industry was humbly grateful.

TO be sure, the expanding power of government over many areas of theoretically private life and business is not unique to Britain. The national tax, credit and fiscal policies of the U.S. government, for instance, intimately affect the conduct and welfare of American business. But there are definite differences, and they all add up to a larger degree of government power, intervention and control in Britain than in the United States.

The differences arise in part from the fact that the government in Britain controls something like 20 per cent of the nation's basic industrial output. After the Labour party won Britain's general election of 1945, the new government bought (from the various private owners) and nationalized the coal, iron and steel, gas, electric power and transport (chiefly railway and trucking) industries. Broadcasting and most scheduled air transport were already government monopolies.

The steel industry was the last to be nationalized, and most of it was returned to private ownership by the Conservative party after it won power in 1951. Part of the trucking industry was also "denationalized." The other nationalized industries were placed in the hands of public corporations, which operate them today on the government's behalf. These corporations are run by boards and commissions made up of former private managers, professional civil servants and distinguished citizens, including labor leaders and retired politicians. The operating bodies are responsible to government ministers, who in turn are responsible to Parliament.

How has nationalization worked? There is no short answer to the question. When the government took them over, the coal and railway industries were run down, short of capital and for the most part poorly managed. Nationalization for them was initially a salvage operation, and as such it has succeeded. The electric power industry has been run well, and the government's bold development of atomic power plants to supplement the expanded system of steam and hydroelectric plants has been outstanding. National operation of the gas industry has been less successful, but nobody appears to quarrel seriously with it.

The question of whether these enterprises show a profit is not always considered a fair yardstick; such social objectives as maintaining maximum employment often outweigh financial considerations. But it is worth noting that the National Coal Board operated the mines at a deficit during seven of its first 12 years and between 1947 and 1962 (when it showed a profit) piled up a deficit of $227 million. The nationalized railways have consistently shown heavy losses, although trucking profits enabled the over-all British Transport Commission to report a surplus in six of its first 11 years and efforts are being made to reorganize the railway system and make it pay. Consumer rates for nationalized gas went up 70 per cent between 1950 and 1962.

PERHAPS the most valid judgment of nationalization is made by the British public. No faction in Britain seriously argues that the presently nationalized industries should be returned to private ownership.

If most of the British are mildly content with the socialist experiment in nationalization, they are downright proud of the public-welfare system that has been developed since the national government took broad responsibility in 1946 for the basic well-being of every man, woman and child in Britain.

Public concern for private welfare in Britain dates back at least to the 16th Century; the most famous early law was the "Poor Relief Act" in 1601, which provided harsh and minimal care for the destitute. From that time well into the present century, destitution was treated as a disgraceful condition calling for only a modicum of relief and no sympathy whatever. Young apprentices recruited by merchants and artisans from the country's charitable institutions were literally worked and beaten to death as recently as a century and a half ago. The great 19th Century novelist, Charles Dickens, derived some of his most harrowing tales from the horrors of public almshouses, or poorhouses.

Important social improvements were introduced during the early decades of this century, and by the 1930s reform had gone a long way. Britain then possessed a variety of welfare services which provided much medical care, emergency relief, unemployment compensation, old-age pensions and the like. But they were uneven from the standpoint both of benefits and of coverage, and some of them were available only on a specific showing of need—what the British call a "means test."

During World War II a study directed by a celebrated social scientist, the late Lord Beveridge, produced a grand design for the complete nationalization and standardization of all of the basic welfare services. It is generally assumed that the Conservative party of Winston Churchill, then the prime minister, would have enacted the leading principles of the famous

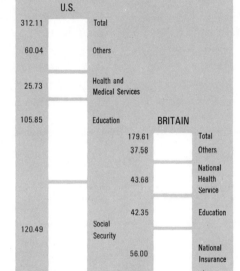

PER CAPITA WELFARE
EXPENDITURES, 1960-1961

U.S.

312.11 Total

60.04   Others

25.73   Health and Medical Services

105.85 Education   BRITAIN

        179.61 Total
        37.58   Others

        43.68   National Health Service

        42.35   Education

120.49 Social Security

        56.00   National Insurance

CHART shows how U.S. and Britain spend welfare funds. Britain spends less per capita but purchasing power of pound is greater.

"womb-to-tomb" Beveridge Report if the Conservatives had won the 1945 general election. But the Labour party won, and the postwar Labour government under Prime Minister Clement Attlee created the national welfare system that exists today.

Britain pays out some $10 billion annually from the government's funds for all of its social services, including education and public housing. About $7 billion of this amount goes into the category of welfare services. The mandatory contributions from employers and workers to medical, unemployment and pension funds make up about $3 billion of the $10 billion total at the present time. An important feature of the British system is that the beneficiaries pay only a small portion of the cost in direct contributions; well over half of the amount needed comes from general tax revenues.

The welfare enterprise of which Britons are proudest is the National Health Service. One reason Britishers are so pleased with what they call "the National Health" or "the N.H.S." is that there is nothing remotely like it in the otherwise envied U.S. Any scrap of news implying that Americans are dying in the streets because they cannot afford medical care (a notion that many Britons find quite believable) is good for a display headline in some of the more sensational London newspapers.

Apart from their exaggerated (though not entirely false) estimate of Americans' medical burdens, the British have ample reason to be proud of their Health Service. Since it came into being in 1948, no resident of Britain has had to worry about the costs of medical and dental care or hospital treatment. This is not to say that the service is completely free, as is widely supposed elsewhere. Because general revenues pay for so much of the program, a family man with two young children who pays an income tax of $965.65 on total earnings of $5,600 a year has good reason to feel that in so doing he is paying handsomely for his public medical care.

But the deduction from wages and salaries for the health service is at present only 37 cents a week for an employed man. The charges for prescriptions, dental treatment and such things as spectacles and hearing aids are still minor. And the few people who are unable to afford the charges can always turn to the government's emergency relief agency, the National Assistance Board, for the necessary money.

PEOPLE who prefer private care can still get it. The number of Britons who buy private medical insurance has jumped 10 times (to more than one million) in recent years. But the vast majority, including many in the upper social and economic groups, rely mainly or entirely on "the National Health." The government medical service, incidentally, permits any citizen to choose or change his physician.

The British Medical Association, which once fought the concept of a nationalized service as fiercely as the American Medical Association resists the mildest beginnings of a similar approach in the U.S., is now to a large extent an administrative arm of the government ministry that supervises the service. British doctors as a group are financially better off under the national service than they were as private practitioners, though they also work harder. The government pays the patients' bills, the average general practitioner or specialist makes more money than he did in the old days, and those who wish to do so are still free to take private patients on the side.

The quality of the service inevitably varies from place to place and from doctor to doctor. Britain sorely needs more and better hospitals, and the government has just begun to build them on something like an adequate scale. But the National Health Service is open to everybody, and it has contributed enormously to both the physical and the psychological well-being of Britain in a period when the country has needed all the lift it can get.

Although Britons are generally happy with their welfare setup, not all is serene with government in Britain. The tremendous growth of governmental responsibilities presents a genuine threat to the parliamentary system. If and when Parliament becomes unable to exercise its constitutional power to keep watch upon and control the British government as a whole, that government will have changed for the worse. There is much evidence that such a change is now occurring.

Christopher Hollis, who for 10 years was a Conservative M.P., expresses the views of many other M.P.s in all parties when he observes that Parliament has been in "headlong decline" since 1945. The ever-growing complexity of domestic government is only one of many reasons for this decline, but it is a very important reason.

MINISTERS and phalanxes of senior civil servants stand between Parliament and the public corporations which run the nationalized industries, and M.P.s despair of closing the gap. The welfare system, good in itself, is too complex and its bureaucratic workings are too remote for the kind of restraining check that Parliament is expected to maintain. Legislation by administrative regulation (executive order) rather than by parliamentary statute grows in volume and scope; there appears to be no other way to enable government to do its necessary business. Both domestic and world pressures compel—or seem to compel—prime ministers and cabinets to concentrate more and more of the effective power of government in their own hands and to share less and less of that power with Parliament, which in constitutional principle possesses most of it.

Thoughtful Britons of every political opinion realize that all of this may be creating a real governmental crisis. Today the British genius for government that produced the parliamentary system in the first place is called upon to save that very system from atrophy.

In an old people's home a 79-year-old pensioner signs over a part of her weekly governmental check to help pay the cost of her keep.

The Guiding Hand of the State

The welfare state that is today's Britain is observed intently by most of the world, for it is a tempered socialism administered largely by conservatives. No Briton need go hungry or, when ill, untreated. Literally from womb to tomb the citizen is under the government's protection. Virtually free medical care begins even before he is born. As an adult he may live in subsidized housing, collect a comfortable allowance when he is jobless, and receive an adequate pension when he is old. And when he dies, he may be buried free of charge. Not only is the individual cared for, but most economic activity is rigidly supervised. Nevertheless, initiative still abounds in Britain, and the country continues to produce its share of inventive and energetic men.

89

THE DOCTOR, *paid by the government, enjoys a good income, but his patients call him more often, and he has had to cut the time he allots to each*

About to give a 78-year-old woman an injection, the doctor boils

AFTER A CALL, the doctor (*left*), a general practitioner, hurries through a yard. He tends about 80 patients a day and has hospital, committee and form-filling work to do.

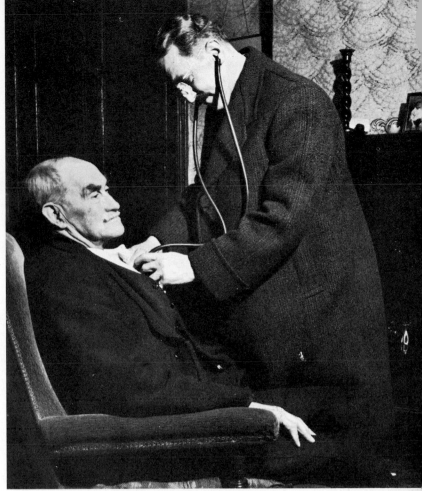

IN A FARMHOUSE, he checks a 77-year-old man who has a bad heart. Many calls are miles from town, and like all doctors he makes some merely to boost morale.

water for his needle. The visit, unusually long, lasted 10 minutes.

IN HIS SURGERY (*right*), he treats a year-old infant for a blistered foot. Though most patients genuinely need aid, some come for such trivia as having their ears cleaned.

ASSEMBLY-LINE EXPERTS put together the turbo-prop Viscount (*above*), which was the first plane of its type to be approved for commercial airline use.

EXPLORER OF THE UNIVERSE, the immense radio telescope (*opposite*) at Jodrell Bank has bounced signals off the moon and has guided U.S. rockets.

PROUD ARTISANS have made Wedgwood china famous all over the world (*right*). The craftsman in the center served in the company for some 60 years.

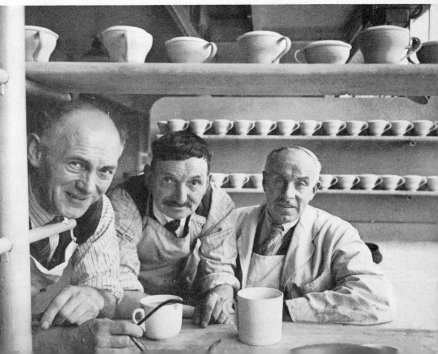

DYNAMIC MEN *with brains can rise to vast power and wealth no matter what their origins, and some have developed vital industries*

PUBLISHER Charles Garrett Ponsonby Moore (*above*) is an earl by heritage, but his success is his own. Once an advertising salesman, he is now the managing director of *The Financial Times*.

PRESS LORD, the late William Ewert Berry, first Viscount Camrose (*opposite*), was born in a mining town, entered journalism, and with his brother Lord Kemsley built up a newspaper chain.

AUTO BUILDER William Edward Rootes, who is now Lord Rootes (*right*), transformed his father's bicycle and motor car agency into the giant Rootes Group for producing and marketing cars.

PHYSICIST Sir John Cockcroft (*above*), founder of Britain's atomic center at Harwell, shared a Nobel Prize in 1951. He is now Master of Churchill College, Cambridge.

BIOCHEMIST Sir Alexander Todd (*left*) explained a key to the function of life-sustaining nucleic acids, whose structure is shown here. He won a Nobel Prize in 1957.

CIVIL SERVANT and the epitome of the dedicated official, Sir Edward Bridges (*opposite*) was Permanent Secretary to the Treasury for 11 years. He is now Lord Bridges.

Members of the newly prospering "upper working class," the Birds take their afternoon tea and cake. As Tina Bird pours for her mother,

Colin (left), Eric Bird, Kevin and Freddy await their turn.

The Happy Birds

WESTON Road in Chiswick, a residential area of outer London, contains a tidy collection of narrow brick houses standing wall-to-wall along the gentle curve of the street. In the vanished age before World War II it was a stronghold of Britain's lower middle class—small shopkeepers and chief clerks, the modest legions to whom a home in one of London's innumerable Weston Roads was a symbol and a confirmation of a cherished status. Above them was a higher middle class and, so far above as to be almost unimaginable, the upper-class gentry and aristocracy. Below them, known and comforting in its visible inferiority of circumstance, was the great British working class. Whether its members lived around the corner in the meaner streets of Chiswick (pronounced Chizzik), in the London tenement districts of St. Pancras and Pimlico, or in the slums of distant Coventry and Wigan, a gulf not measurable in blocks or miles separated them from Weston Road. It was the gulf between salary and wage, black coat and overalls, pen and hammer, home and 'ome. It was not impassable: many in prewar Weston Road had found the way there by night school, apprenticeship and painful heed to the proprieties of speech and demeanor. But their advent was a signal to themselves and others that they were no longer of the working class and never had been in spirit.

IN the 1950s, a profound change occurred in Weston Road. Its nature cannot be seen from the narrow sidewalks. The bits of fenced green space in front of the houses, the prim curtains and the window boxes look the same as ever. The street has not deteriorated; here is no declining neighborhood. The change is to be found inside—behind the door, for example, of No. 56 Weston Road.

This is the home of Mr. and Mrs. Eric Bird and their four children: Christina, nearing 16; Frederick George Harry, 14 (born on the same day as Prince Charles); Colin, nine; and Kevin, six. The head of the household, Eric Bird, is a stocky, solid-seeming man, mildly spoken but with strong views. He was a workingman when he moved to Weston Road and he will be of the working class and proud of it until he dies. He and his jolly wife, Lily, still speak in the broad dialect of Lancashire, where they were born 40 and 39 years ago, respectively, in the industrial town of Oldham.

The great change they personify is not only that they are in Weston Road but that they belong and are accepted there—without change in themselves as people. When Eric Bird finished his war service as a soldier in Britain and India and went back to work for around $20 a week in 1946, he could not have afforded a home in Weston Road and in any case would not have dreamed of moving there: he was working class, and Weston Road was middle class. If by chance he and his family had turned up there, in the 1940s, the neighborhood would have been said to be "going down."

In the more fluid and prosperous Britain of today, however, Weston Road has if anything gone up economically, with the coming of the Birds and other wage-earners of their class, and in community atmosphere it has not declined socially. Few if any of Weston Road's prewar residents would have equaled Eric Bird's current weekly income of $60 or better, and they would have been appalled if asked to pay his weekly rent of $10. He probably earns more than some of his salaried middle-class neighbors do even now, but that is not the main point. The main point is that in the 1960s the working-class Birds, without pretending to be what they are not, can fit comfortably into the life of Britain's Weston Roads.

"It's a laugh!" the Birds would say if someone were to tell them they represent anything other than their happy selves. But they do. They represent a new "upper working class" that is nearer to personifying the Britain of the 1960s than the upper-class Englishmen who constitute the conventional British image.

Eric Bird is a skilled machinist and aircraft fitter who has risen to be a supervisor of other workmen assembling fuselages for the firm of Vickers-Armstrongs in a plant some 20 miles from Chiswick. His basic wage for a 42-hour week is approximately $34. But these figures are meaningless to him; his actual wage, with overtime and bonuses for fast work, is seldom less than $60 and occasionally nearer $70.

AS a fitter he worked with overtime on Mondays, Tuesdays and Thursdays from 8 a.m. to 7:30 p.m., with an hour out for midday dinner and 15 minutes for afternoon tea; on Wednesdays and Fridays, without overtime, from 8 a.m. to 5 or 5:30 p.m.; on Saturdays from 8 to 12:30 at time-and-a-half; and, when he could, on Sundays from 8 to 12:30 at double time. Now he works overtime only on weekends, partly because with his increased base pay as a supervisor he is less dependent on extra work and partly because a battered motorcycle he rode to and from the plant wore out and now he must catch a ride home whenever an accommodating friend is ready to leave.

In a typical week he may gross some $62. From this is withheld the equivalent of 75 cents in income tax and $2.15 (including a recent increase) for his direct contribution to the public welfare programs which provide, among other things, medical care for him and his family, compensation when he is sick or unemployed and a pension when he is old. With $58 in take-home pay, he feels that he is doing quite well. And because prices and costs are low in Britain compared with those in the U.S., Eric Bird has done better than a straight pound-dollar conversion of his earnings (the pound is worth $2.80) would make it seem to Americans. Everything considered, $58 a week means to Eric Bird about what $100 would mean to a comparable American worker.

WHAT it chiefly means for the family at No. 56 Weston Road is a degree of comfort that they could not have imagined 15 years ago. Eric Bird says that with the considerable postwar inflation he is no better off on his $58 than he was then on $20; an economist would say that $58 buys what about $35 would have bought in 1946. All around Bird at home, however, is evidence that the difference between his wage then and in 1963 cannot be measured solely by price indexes.

It is partly a matter of atmosphere: Lily Bird and the children are well dressed, well fed, happy —and *confident*. Recalling that in his boyhood he was lucky to have fourpence a week for spending, the master of the house says with embarrassed pride that each of his younger children gets two shillings a week (28 cents)—plus a little more from the indulgent Lily. She earns $10.50 a week from a part-time job at a neighborhood nursery school.

The Birds have no bathtub, telephone or central heat; they do have an inside toilet. But their small and characteristically packed living room contains a piano for Tina, a "telly," or television set, and a three-tiered aquarium assembled by Eric Bird. There is a new set of bedroom furniture, bought like the "telly" on "hire-purchase" installments and already paid for. Unusually prudent, the Birds always limit their installment commitments to around three dollars a week.

The Birds just about live up to what the head of the house earns—or, as he puts it, he works up to what they need. Eric and Lily Bird never visit a pub and seldom go to a movie. Their success has made home for them an all-binding place, pleasant and attractive. The pubs used to draw many workingmen in search of some measure of relief from the depressing grime and poverty of home. Now, for such as Eric Bird, home is nicer than any pub.

Eric Bird's war service in Asia gave him an otherwise unsatisfied taste for travel, and the thing he misses most is a really good vacation trip now and then. In dreamy moments he says that if he made a pot in the football pools, he would take the family abroad. But for him and Lily the extent of travel is an occasional return to Oldham.

Mrs. Bird worked in an ammunition factory during the war, and her husband tolerates her present part-time job at the nursery. But the day he came home from the war he insisted that she cease full-time work. "I think a woman's got enough to do at 'ome," he says with genial firmness. "All I ever do is wash," Lily Bird says quite happily, summing up her full days of housework, shopping and walking to and from her work at the nursery. In the evenings, when Eric Bird has returned and had his supper, the little living room is in a warm turmoil, with children studying or watching television, the young ones climbing over their father on the sofa, Lily perhaps sewing in a corner. The Birds are utterly without "side" and the pains of social ambition, but in small ways they share every Britisher's unceasing concern with the accent and manners of his children. "Don't say h'orange —say *orange*," Lily will say to Kevin, opening her mouth wide as if expelling the superfluous letter.

ALTHOUGH the welfare state and its benefits are very real to them, the Birds do not feel beholden to the state. They consider that they pay for what they get and expect to get. Eric Bird is aware, for one thing, that the basic weekly welfare deduction from his pay is the same for every regular earner, and that it would be relatively more of a bite if he were thrown back to the old $20 or even to the national average wage of $43.

At present only 38 cents of the $2.15 deducted for welfare every week goes for "the National Health," but it is this service that has meant most to the Birds. During a two-month period while Tina was still at school, Colin was treated for wasp stings, had five stitches taken in a cut leg, and spent several days in a hospital after he lost the tips of two fingers in a swinging gate. He also had five baby teeth extracted and his tonsils removed. Tina was hit in the eye by an air-gun pellet, requiring X rays at a hospital, and was ill with pleurisy at home for two weeks. Freddy was treated for chronic pains in his legs. These misadventures cost Father Bird only 14 cents for each prescription (today each would cost 28 cents). Children's dental treatment is free, but most adults pay modest sums for dentures and work not considered strictly necessary. Eric Bird does not share the widespread resentment against these charges. He feels they were necessary in order to curb the excessive demands which overwhelmed doctors when the service began in 1948.

DOCTORS are still extremely busy, but the Birds say that they have received adequate, prompt and courteous treatment. On office calls to their neighborhood physician's crowded office, the wait can be tedious. But their doctor answered the night call for Tina's pleurisy within an hour, and he had the unlucky Colin quickly admitted to a hospital in his time of need. Eric Bird compares all of this favorably with his boyhood in Oldham. Merely to see a doctor used to cost the equivalent of $1.80, he remembers, "and we just didn't go." Even so, Eric Bird has learned from experience that "I can't really afford to be ill." After four days at home with gastritis, he "crept back to work" before he had fully recovered. His employer pays no sick leave, and the maximum $27.50 that the state would have paid had he been out a week seemed far too little for his needs.

All of the children except Tina arrived "on the National Health." Her birth and Mrs. Bird's hospital confinement cost Eric Bird about $45, or more than he then earned in two weeks. The younger children were born at home, a locale which Mrs. Bird prefers to a free hospital because "when you're home you can have friends in and have a cup of tea when you like." For not patronizing the overburdened hospital system, Mrs. Bird received a special state grant of $14 on each occasion—plus the standard $35 which every mother gets when a child is born.

Mrs. Bird is entitled to go to the post office each week and draw her "family allowance" of $3.92 ($1.12 for Freddy, $1.40 each for Colin and Kevin; nothing for Tina, the first child). By law this money is the mother's. Like the nursery-school earnings, it is treated in the Bird household as something extra, and Eric Bird does not take it into account in his tight budget.

IF Eric Bird retires at 65, he will receive a basic government pension of around $19 a week if Lily is alive, or about $9 if he is alone. If he works until he is 70, he will get about $18 or $12. If Eric dies first, Lily can expect a widow's pension of between $9 and $19 a week, varying with the number of dependent children. These standard benefits can be supplemented by direct relief from "the National Assistance" on a showing of need. But, like all of their class, the Birds hate anything resembling a means test and have an ingrained horror of relief.

Eric and Lily Bird finished elementary school in Oldham and went to work when they were 14, the "leaving age" at that time for the vast majority of British children. If they had been exceptionally bright and their parents had been unusually ambitious for them, they might have had more schooling, and Eric might even have attended a university on a scholarship. But they were not among the few of their class and time who made the strenuous effort necessary. Now the government requires the Eric Birds' children to stay in school until they are 15, and encourages them to stay longer. If qualified, they may stay through university level, at public expense.

British society as a whole, however, is still geared to the assumption that most children either do not want, or are not qualified for a formal education much beyond the age of 15 or 16. In a time of rising aspiration and of tremendous public effort and expenditure to satisfy it, the elder Birds seem quite happy with the traditional assumption. They were pleased when Tina got a job at 15; they naturally expect her to marry in due course. With 14-year-old Freddy, it was different. As he neared the usual school "leaving age" of 15, his father urged him to choose a trade and to plan to learn it at night school or in a full-time apprenticeship. Freddy, weary of schooling, just wanted to get a job. This worried Eric Bird who told his son: "If you've served an apprenticeship or been to night school and you've got a trade, it stands to reason that you've got an advantage over the next man." The experience and convictions of a lifetime gave force to his view that "a man needs a trade."

Eric Bird would have advised his son to learn a trade at any time. But there was a special urgency in the period when Freddy was approaching 15. British unemployment was high. From a total of 399,000 in 1961, less than 2 per cent of the nation's work force, it had increased to nearly 900,000, or almost 4 per cent, in early 1963. The worst of it was in Northern Ireland, northern England, Wales and Scotland; southern England, where the Birds lived, remained relatively well off. But the Birds noticed that Tina had a little more trouble than they expected when she sought a job.

ERIC BIRD was fairly confident, but not so confident as he would have been a year earlier, that when Freddy's time came he could find a job with or without training for a trade. As for his own job, Eric Bird told himself that the aircraft industry was less liable to a slump than shipbuilding, for instance. But he also knew that "it depends on government orders for aircraft, and orders can be cancelled." His four-day illness had reminded him and the family of how close they were to the edge of stringency, if not of downright want. The Birds still had their sense of affluence, and the confidence that came from years of steady work. But, for the first time since they had moved to Weston Road, there was a touch of anxiety in their talk. Eric Bird was heard to say, "You never know."

LIFE and hope for the Birds have narrowed in several respects. Jouncing to and from work on his old motorcycle a few years ago, Eric Bird looked forward to buying a small motor car. When the tired bike finally "packed up," he discovered that he would do well to find the money for a new motorcycle (he has in mind a Model 650 Triumph Thunderbird, big and powerful enough for a sidecar in which to haul the family on weekend trips). He also had dreamed of buying the Weston Road house if it were ever available for purchase. Now the down payment, not to mention the total price of around $2,800, seems to be even farther from his reach than a motor car.

In the main, however, Eric Bird is still his sturdy self: a Briton who knows his mind and how to speak it. Although his enthusiasm for labor unions is distinctly limited, he is a Labour party man by choice and origin. The typical Conservative, he says with emphasis, "is a rich man, and no rich man is a friend of mine." A fine craftsman himself, he has no patience with what he regards as the low working standards of the day. "Years ago," he says, "the idea was, more or less, better work. A man tried to be as good in his trade as the old fellow who taught him. Nowadays he does his work good enough to pass the inspection."

As an intelligent and perceptive citizen, Eric Bird is all too aware that things have not gone well for Britain in the world. The fact that many countries of Europe have passed Britain in their rates of economic growth and their relative levels of prosperity is especially galling. Eric Bird speaks for his countrymen when he says: "It saddens me that we've come down in the world a bit. Look at Germany and France and all those countries—going great guns. It's got a bit of a feeling of stalemate over here."

NOBLE OWNERS of 16th Century Burghley House (*left*), the Marquess and Marchioness of Exeter, inspect a decorated wall in one of the rooms of state.

RED SALON of Ragley Hall (*opposite*) provides a quiet haven for the present Marquess of Hertford and his wife when the visiting public has left.

A Narrowing of the Social Gap

As the workingman's comfort and security have increased, the lot of Britain's well-to-do, especially the hereditary landowners, has become more difficult. Staggering inheritance taxes have made it hard for even Britain's oldest and proudest noble families to retain their ancestral homes, and many have had to open their houses to the fee-paying public or sell off their art collections. Although some new fortunes have been made by vigorous businessmen, large incomes are subject to extremely stiff taxes. But the degrading poverty too common in Britain as recently as the 1930s has largely disappeared, and the national life has taken on new health and vigor.

OLD-TIME NANNIES, who used to be the status symbols of the middle class, still wheel "prams" in the parks of London. But today only the rich can afford them, and the ones shown above belong to a vanishing breed.

MODERN MOTHERS, who live in new suburban housing developments like the one shown at right, have neither the money nor the room for servants. One result is a much closer relationship between the parents and children.

QUIET PLEASURES survive despite the changes, and few are more stubbornly cherished by middle-class folk than a holiday at Bath, with morning coffee to music (*opposite*). Bath was once a haunt of kings bent on privacy.

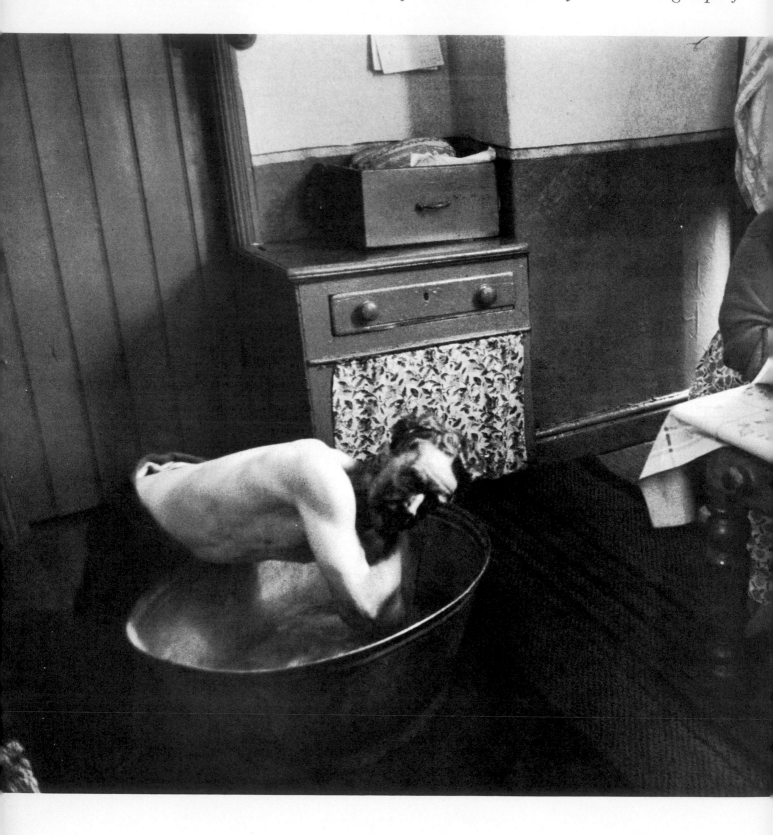

long-underprivileged workers

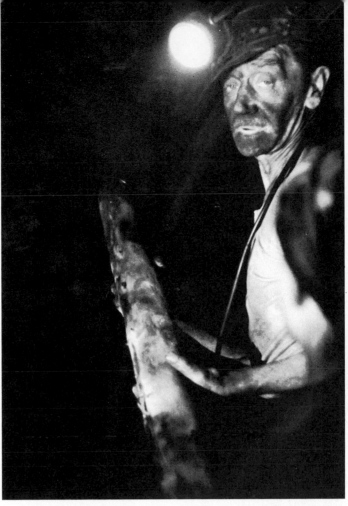

BELOW GROUND, James shows other coal miners how to shore up a gallery roof. A mine worker since he was 14, James does a job reserved for men too old to dig.

AT HOME, James washes off the mine dirt in a tub of hot water (*left*). The James' son went to college and Mrs. James is happy that he has not become a miner.

AT HIS CLUB, which is for miners only, James (*left, in foreground*) plays a game of darts. Since nationalization miners' wages and working conditions have improved.

Millionaire television producer Honoria Plesch (left background) entertains her brother (background) and nephews at the heated,

indoor swimming pool in her home in London's Kensington area.

The New Affluence

EVERYWHERE in Britain in the late 1950s there were signs of an astonishing and unprecedented condition of prosperity that came to be called "the New Affluence." The condition was especially remarkable in that it followed directly upon the years of postwar austerity.

The outward marks of this phenomenon were both social and economic. They ranged from monster traffic jams in the cities to large signs urging Britons to DRINKA PINTA MILKA DAY. They included hordes of tight-trousered young men and smartly dressed girls darting through the night streets of London to coffee bars, milk bars and jazz clubs—and 460,000 people thronging to view an exhibition of Picasso paintings. This prosperity brought with it a new leisure, and a saving measure of relief from the tensions that accompanied Britain's decline as a world power. But above all it was new and exciting in a very special way.

Affluence as such was hardly new to Britain, which had been the world's richest nation in the last century and for part of this one. What was new was a general well-being that permeated all classes. Almost everybody, not merely the rich and privileged, shared the prosperity of the 1950s to some degree. Britain's earlier periods of prosperity had been founded upon a low-wage economy in which a living standard barely above the subsistence level was assumed to be the natural lot of most people. A peaceful social and political revolt against this conception had been in process since the Industrial Revolution, continuing through the 19th Century and reaching a climax with the election of the Labour party in 1945. Labour went out of power after six years, but when a combination of factors—including a prodigious effort to increase British exports and a relaxation of credit controls—brought an economic upturn in the 1950s, the masses of ordinary people were at last in a position to claim some of the rewards.

THE over-all result was a profound social revolution in popular tastes, aspirations and habits. The revolution is more important for Britain's future social structure than the partial nationalization of industry and the expansion of national welfare services that preceded it.

In the early 1960s there were cruel reminders that affluence has to be earned. The plain fact was that too many affluent Britons were taking more out of their economy than they put into it in the form of efficient work. By comparison with the performances of such continental countries as France and Germany, the total value of work done and goods produced in Britain grew at a dismally low annual rate (in recent times, never more than 2.5 per cent a year and occasionally as little as 1 per cent). Despite the postwar construction of many new plants and the introduction of modern processes, Britain still suffered from a deadening residue of outmoded factories, equipment and work practices. Most of the improvement had occurred in the favored south of England, too little of it in the chronic "depressed areas" of northern England, Scotland, Wales and Northern Ireland. These and other factors finally brought about a drop in business

and an alarming increase in unemployment. Britons suddenly realized that they had no guarantee that the happy condition of the recent past would last forever. But, notwithstanding all of this, it was clear in the early 1960s that the social consequences of the great upsurge were permanent. In terms of what the British people not only wanted but expected to have and keep, the new affluence had come to stay.

Every economic indicator was up. In 12 years, the average weekly industrial wage for men more than doubled, going from $21 to $43.80. Personal income also more than doubled. The amount of money spent on such major items as motor cars, furniture and refrigerators trebled —though prices were up, too. The number of houses built for private owners went up from 34,320 in 1952 to 180,727 in 1961. One in every 2.5 families had a motor car in 1962, compared with one in seven in 1951, and the total number of private cars almost trebled, jumping from 2.3 million to nearly six million. The number of home television sets increased from 344,000 in 1950 to more than 12 million in mid-1962.

But these figures barely begin to measure the change in national wants and habits. A 1958 survey of 200 working-class homes in the industrial town of Morley showed both the nature of the change and the low living level at which it had started. Only three of 200 Morley homes had bathtubs, only six had running hot water and only four had inside toilets—but 125 had television sets.

FOREIGN travel, once largely confined to middle- and upper-income groups, is now enjoyed by wage earners too. More than three million Britons go abroad annually on vacation, compared with 1.2 million in 1947. "Abroad" in British parlance means anywhere away from the main island, and many of the travelers still go no farther than Ireland or the Channel Islands off the French coast. But two thirds visit the European continent and the rest of the world, and a large number of the new travelers are working-class people. A wry joke among some middle-class housewives today is that they must take their holidays at Britain's seaside resorts while their servants—if they still have servants—go to France and Switzerland.

If there is one social and economic group that feels worse rather than better off, it is this salaried middle class. Here it must be explained that even in today's affluent Britain the levels of pay are uncomfortably low by U.S. standards—even allowing for a considerable gap in prices between the two countries. A university graduate going into business management is lucky to start at $2,300 a year and will be doing quite well if by the time he is 30 he is earning $4,300 a year. The government's senior civil servants are considered to be extremely well paid at $12,000 to $14,000, a salary level arrived at to equal comparable grades in industry. The great divide between lower- and upper-income levels is still $5,600. When 627,000 Britons reported taxable incomes of $5,600 or more in 1961—an increase of 307,000 in three years—it was a sign that affluence had spread appreciably.

SEVERAL steps to lighten taxes, notably a change from $5,600 to $14,000 as the point at which surtaxes on earned income start, have somewhat relieved the financial pressure on middle-income Britons. But the pinch that hurts most comes from the pressure of a widening social competition. The precious symbols of class status—private schooling for the children, a house in the country or in a "decent" suburb, vacation trips abroad—become ever more expensive and at the same time ever less distinctive in themselves as the number of Britons competing for the same symbols and status steadily increases.

What matters in the end is not so much privilege in itself as a *sense* of privilege—of living and being better than those one social rung below. To many Britons born into the middle classes, the new affluence seems to be principally a vast scheme to deflate and diminish their cherished status. But these are the incidental pains of a changing society. Even the put-upon middle class is better off in many respects than it used to be.

Perhaps the flashiest symptom of the new affluence is the increased number of millionaires—or of people who live like millionaires. And by this is meant millionaires in *pounds*—those who possess $2,800,000, the dollar equivalent of £1,000,000. Mere *dollar* millionaires would hardly be worth notice in today's Britain.

Defining a millionaire is not simple: there are many ways to earn and to own capital. A loose definition of a British "millionaire," as the term is used here, is anyone whose income equals the £6,000 that may be netted after taxes from £1,000,000 invested in stocks and bonds. In 1949, one hundred British taxpayers had incomes of £6,000 or more after taxes; 12 years later the number was 15,000. Just a rung below were 50,000 taxpayers who in 1961 had incomes after taxes of £4,000 to £6,000. Their number had shot up from only 5,100 ten years earlier.

But the actual number of people in Britain who spend money as if they *were* millionaires is much larger than the number of high-rate taxpayers indicates. Thanks to company expense accounts, credit and, above all, that notable British device, the tax-exempt capital gain, thousands live on a scale that their particular salaries and other taxed income could not of themselves possibly support.

EXPENSE accounts work in Britain more or less as they do in the U.S. and elsewhere. The Board of Inland Revenue, once very lenient, has considerably tightened its rules and restrictions. But company cars for personal use are still routine. Expensive, hard-to-get town apartments for executives who live in the country are often provided at company expense. If country homes can be shown to have some business use, part of their upkeep may also be a company charge. Many an item labeled "entertainment" on an expense account has concealed the expenses of an executive's mistress.

A particularly gaudy example of expense-account abuse became public knowledge some years ago when the company that manufactures Daimler automobiles threw out its flamboyant chairman, Sir Bernard Docker. He and his spectacular wife, who regarded herself as very much a figure in the company management, were accused of putting on the expense account such items as two gold-plated Daimler cars, one of them upholstered in zebra skins, and a $22,000 outfit for Lady Docker that included a gold lamé dress, a mink cape and a mink-trimmed hat. Sir Bernard finally paid for the clothes, but the company directors and shareholders decided that he had definitely overdone a good thing and gave him the sack.

THE big bonanza, however, is the capital gain. In the United States, long-term capital gains (the profits realized on selling an investment) are narrowly defined and are generally taxed up to 25 per cent. British income that is defined as capital gain is not taxed at all, although the justice of this is being widely disputed in Britain. Some profits, such as those on stocks and bonds held longer than six months after purchase, and those on sporting bets, are capital gains by fixed rule and are never taxed. Many others are exempt only if they are deemed to lie outside the individual's regular line of business. Thus a merchant who has owned his residence for at least three years and then sells it can count on the profit being listed as a capital gain and not taxed. If he sells a second and then a third house, however, the authorities may conclude that he is in the real estate business and tax his profits. Even so, some of the most spectacular tax-free gains of recent years have been made in real estate.

A classic case of capital-gain definition involved a speculator who some years ago bought one million rolls of surplus army toilet paper, resold them for a huge profit, and claimed that his gain was tax-free because he had never previously dealt in that commodity. The tax authorities and a court held that one million rolls put him in the business, first time or not, and he had to pay a high tax. A Royal Commission of inquiry which looked into this and other

cases concluded that the exemption of capital gains from taxation led to some abuses, but nevertheless should be continued under an improved system of review, so as not to discourage individual saving and investment.

With its built-in temptation to deceive the tax authorities if possible, the exemption of capital gains is one of many things that encourage the national disease of "fiddling." Crudely defined, fiddling is any form of cheating on taxes that the individual can get away with. In its finer forms, it involves a degree of adroitness that is supposed to redeem it from being classed as downright dishonesty. Grosser forms of fiddling, such as major expense-account abuses and tax evasion, are more common than Britons like to admit. The prevalence and toleration of fiddling have induced a general cynicism among the British people that is one of the less attractive aspects of the new affluence.

New-rich magnates are not new to Britain: many 19th Century industrialists, for example, were rewarded for their work by being ennobled by the Crown, and a large proportion of the current members of the House of Lords have titles that date back only a few generations. Postwar Britain, however, has produced some unusually gaudy examples of the self-made rich, who are interesting in part because they represent important trends of the new affluence.

ONE such tycoon is Charles Clore, a graying multimillionaire whose father was a textile merchant in the slums of London's Whitechapel district. Clore went to work in the family business at 15, and turned his first speculative profit when he was 21. He later proved to be Britain's outstanding "raider" of established companies, buying control of them out from under the noses of the old managements. Because he has demonstrated that he can put assets to work and boost efficiency, he is regarded today as a respected power in shipbuilding, hosiery machinery, shoe manufacturing, structural steel and electronics. He turned the handsome profit of $11,760,000 in one maneuver alone, the formation of a holding company.

Clore has to some degree also made his way into the higher strata of London society. No less a personage than the Duchess of Kent attended one of his parties—a feather in the cap of any host—and a number of peers and peeresses have entertained him and have been his guests at his elegant London house. In 1960 Clore joined forces with Jack Cotton, a wealthy real estate speculator and developer. Together they entered the American market as buyers and backers of office buildings.

AN indication of the large sums that the most affluent Britons have available for current spending is provided by Major Alfred Allnatt, a shy multimillionaire who made his fortune as a building contractor. A collector of paintings, he paid more than $1.8 million for six pictures in 1960. In 1959 Major Allnatt headed a syndicate that paid $770,000 for *The Adoration of the Magi*, a Rubens painting that was among the properties sold to raise $30 million in death duties on the estate of the late Duke of Westminster. The present duke's family personifies the survival of inherited wealth and privilege in Britain. Despite confiscatory death duties and high income taxes, this family still owns more than 300 acres in the heart of London. New riches may buy admission to the circles into which the Dukes of Westminster were born, but money alone never buys real acceptance there. That usually takes at least a generation or two.

Lord Marks is a second-generation tycoon, the son of a Polish immigrant who in 1884 opened up a Penny Bazaar in Leeds that expanded into the department-store chain of Marks and Spencer, Ltd. Customers from the top to the bottom of the social structure shop at the chain's 237 stores for high-grade goods at low prices ($30 for a woman's tailored suit of excellent quality, for instance). Many other stores and chains cater to affluent Britain's expanded mass market, but Marks and Spencer did much to foster that market and still leads the way in making profits from it. Between 1946 and 1960 its gross business increased from $50 million to more than $400 million.

Upper-class women boast in a kind of inverted snobbery that they buy their clothes "at Marks and Spencer's." Several peers of the realm are reported to buy their underclothes there. Lord Marks, who was made a baron in 1961 and is chairman of the firm, once said that he aimed to offer everyone "a little bit of luxury, to make a factory girl look like a debutante." This sounds like a publicity man's effusion, but exactly that has happened. Factory girls not only are able to buy good clothes cheaply but have the pleasure of knowing that a nearby shopper could be a duchess.

One of the new Britain's most revealing manifestations is commercial television. Since 1955, the year the government reluctantly authorized its existence in competition with the television programming of the official British Broadcasting Corporation, commercial television has produced a crop of new millionaires and further enriched several old ones. It has vastly stimulated the national mass market and generally enlivened an already lively British scene. And, to the nation's delighted amazement, commercial competition has driven the once stuffy BBC, which carries no advertising, to liven up its fare. Many BBC programs now out-draw their money-making rival.

THE commercial setup is a complex affair which seemingly only the British could have invented. Fifteen private companies licensed by and under contract to a supervising government agency, the Independent Television Authority, prepare the programs and broadcast them over government-controlled transmitters. Each of these companies enjoys a commercial monopoly of specified listening areas at specified times. Two contractors may share a rich audience-area such as London or the industrial Midlands, but only one of them broadcasts at a given time. Each is restricted to a maximum of eight hours of commercial broadcasting in every 24.

Advertisers buy time from the contractors, paying as much as $7,560 a minute for spot commercials in the premium London area on Sunday evenings. But time is *all* they buy: they do not sponsor programs in the American sense and have nothing whatever to do with them. The advertisers are allowed to write their own commercials, but even these are under the contractors' control and strict ITA supervision. A government commission recently decided that commercial television had seriously abused its privileges, and as a result the ITA's supervisory powers were considerably strengthened.

Whether this system has preserved the British public from cultural debasement, as it was intended to do, is highly doubtful. The number of American whodunits and westerns shown suggests that the protected British public is not much better off in this respect than U.S. viewers are. The supervisory trade association of the program contractors has had to warn advertisers against inciting children to "ask Mommy" for advertised goods and thereby "make themselves a nuisance to other people." The same association found it necessary to rule as follows: "We do not suggest that children in commercials should always appear to be little angels, but perhaps steps could be taken during production

to see that their behavior is reasonably civilized."

The system's monopoly feature and the avid demand of advertisers for the limited commercial time have greatly enriched such founders of the industry as Norman Collins, a novelist and former BBC executive who sparked a long fight for official acceptance of commercial television. Collins' original 1955 investment of $5,600 in one of the prosperous London companies was worth $1.4 million in 1958 and has increased in value since that time. His company reported a 1960 profit before taxes of $15 million, and its London competitor did even better (nearly $22 million in profits) in 1960. Tightened public control and the great improvement of BBC programing, however, have lately taken some of the bloom off the industry.

BRITAIN'S advertisers, newly conscious of a growing and changing mass market, spend more than $1.3 billion a year in various media—almost twice their expenditure in 1952. The promotion of quality goods and household appliances, once addressed to a limited middle- and upper-class market, is now directed in the main at what advertising men deliberately try not to think of any more as "the working class."

Blatant snob appeal is apparent in much of the popular advertising. But it is snob appeal aimed at people on the way up rather than at people who are already up and need no assurances to that effect. A motor-car dealer in a London suburb advertises, "You don't only buy a car, you acquire status." The prestigious *Times* of London, a paper which used to take its own and its readers' high position for granted, now keys its promotion to the line, "Top People read *The Times*"—thus emphasizing its value as a status symbol to potential readers hungry for such blessings. The publicity man for one of Britain's new industrial towns asserts, "We are a working town, not a working class town."

The public-relations business, completely scorned 10 years ago, is up and jumping. Some informed Britishers attribute the Conservative party's 1959 election victory in substantial part to the public-relations guidance of Colman,

---

A SAMPLING OF BBC TELEVISION

A typical Saturday of British noncommercial television would include such programs as those listed below. The number of drama and sport programs reflects the BBC's recent efforts to broaden its popular appeal.

12:25 TELEWELE
A children's show in Welsh
12:50 NEWYDDION
News in Welsh
12:55 NOTICE BOARD
1:00 GRANDSTAND
A four-hour program of live and film coverage of a boxing match, horse racing, ice hockey, a rugby game and a swimming match
5:00 THE BOSS CAT
A cartoon show for children
5:25 ZERO ONE
Series drama involving police and badmen
5:50 THE NEWS AND SPORTS
6:00 JUKE BOX JURY
A panel show discussing popular music
6:30 DIXON OF DOCK GREEN
Series drama about London policemen
7:15 LARAMIE
A western film series made in America
8:00 THE RAG TRADE
Series drama about garment industry employees
8:25 THE SATURDAY FILM
A popular movie, often American
9:30 THE NEWS AND THE WEATHER MAN
10:00 SATURDAY SPORT
10:25 THAT WAS THE WEEK THAT WAS
A variety show of satirical comment on the news

Prentis and Varley, a big advertising firm which popularized the campaign slogan, "Life's Better With the Conservatives—Don't Let Labour Ruin It." Colman, Prentis and Varley and its numerous public-relations competitors are not in themselves unusual. What is extraordinary is their growing acceptance and use in recent years by British business firms and public institutions that once held the whole idea and function of public relations to be beneath contempt. In addition to the specialized counsel and services provided by independent agencies, most firms of any size now have their own public-relations officer, often a man who would be perfectly at home on New York's Madison Avenue.

THE new affluence has had a great though somewhat contradictory impact on British sports, the area of national life that interests and involves more people than any other. Attendance at professional soccer games ("Association Football"), long the favorite spectator sport of the British working class, dropped from 41 million in 1950 to 28 million in 1962. But participant sports once reserved to the upper classes—riding, fencing, skiing, sailing, even mountain climbing—attracted an unprecedented number and variety of Britons. An official study called *Sport and the Community* explained that "young people now have more money and leisure and can break into activities which were formerly open only to the well-to-do."

The same study treated dancing as a sport and observed that it "is probably the physical activity which attracts more people of both sexes and ages [*sic*] than any other." It is estimated elsewhere that probably five million Britons go dancing at public halls every week, an increase of two million since 1951.

More and more people, especially the younger ones, are said to be playing various games instead of paying to watch others play them. But a 1960 Gallup Poll tended to confirm the suspicion of some observers that a surprising number of the newly affluent adult Britons, great sports lovers though they are alleged to be, have only a passive interest in games. Asked what they would most like to do with a pleasant Saturday afternoon in summer, a majority of those polled voted for a good sleep. Visiting the seaside was next in preference; watching some sport was a poor third. Actually playing a game only ranked fifth in the recorded replies.

Apart from the fact that it is still popular, there isn't anything for an outsider to say about the peculiarly English game of cricket. There never has been.

Odd though the fact may seem in the country that originated Puritanism, gambling on sports events rates as a major British sport in itself. The nation's regular gamblers include Queen Elizabeth, who generally wagers a couple of pounds on every horse race she watches. It is officially estimated that three out of every four British adults gamble at least occasionally on horse races, dog races (currently down in popularity) or the increasingly popular football pools, in which bets of as little as two cents are placed at long odds on possible winning combinations, and which have been known to pay off in amounts as high as $700,000. A new law permitting bookies to open betting offices anywhere, instead of just at a track, gave a 4 per cent boost to gambling on the horses in 1962, and the total of money wagered exceeded even the stupendous $2.1 billion which Britons bet in 1961. The liberal Betting and Gaming Act also prompted the opening of more than 50 new gambling houses, some of them very opulent and frankly catering only to clients able to lose at least $3,000 a night.

THE Queen's sports-loving consort, the Duke of Edinburgh, has stimulated an unexpected popular interest in polo. Large crowds flock to see it played, although it is still much too expensive to rank as a participant sport. In the Britain of the new affluence, this may not continue to be true. The day conceivably may come when the British workingman doffs his factory clothes at a convenient afternoon hour, motors to the nearest polo ground in his new automobile, and calls for his pony and mallet in a cultured and probably insufferable accent.

The Joys of Leisure

The crowds who fill British dance halls six nights a week consist mostly of typists, office boys, clerks and factory hands. But their new prosperity permits them to spend $100 million a year in these dimly lit, faintly perfumed ballrooms. There they savor the joy of life which other Britons find in the theater and opera, in ritualistic sports or in a holiday by the sea.

118

IN A BALLROOM at Tottenham (*above*), young people converse in low tones between dances. The management forbids blue jeans and enforces a strict dignity.

AT THE OPERA, Lord David Cecil (*right, at foot of stairs*) escorts two ladies up a staircase at Covent Garden. Opera-going is still a leading British social activity.

THE YOUNGER GENERATION *brings new modes and manners to ancient London institutions, transforming their look and mood*

BOOK AND BEARD are in style at the Troubadour (*opposite*), a coffee house where conversation by candlelight is a favorite pastime. Like Americans of the same age, youthful Britons flock to the coffee houses and milk bars.

CIDER AND TALK on a Sunday morning provide some quiet relaxation for two secretaries, lolling at the threshold of a 400-year-old pub. Their informal garb would have been unthinkable for Britons a generation or two earlier.

TOP HATS are worn by many onlookers at Lord's, the famous London cricket ground. Spectators attend some special matches in old-fashioned coaches.

CHAMPAGNE SUPPER on the lawn at Glyndebourne (*right*) makes a pleasant intermission for patrons of Britain's best-known summer operatic festival.

ELEGANT GOWNS worn by aristocratic debutantes (*opposite*) adorn such festivities as a formal ball at the Duke of Bedford's estate, Woburn Abbey.

APPRAISING THE CONTEST from a barge, a St. John's College student, correct in blazer, boater and white flannels, follows the race through a spyglass. But most of his fellows devote themselves to their guests, who by Eights Week custom are sisters or other relatives, rather than girl friends. Colleges have their own barges at the event.

FASHIONABLE FUN *in*
the traditional manner prevails
during Eights Week at
Oxford, when eight-man crews
race their shells on the Isis and
young Britons exhibit a
properly restrained enthusiasm

RACING THE RACERS, rooters who eschew the barges run along the river's edge to cheer their boats on (*right*). Even the fastest can barely keep up with the shells.

MASS ENJOYMENT *is found at Blackpool, a resort that annually jams in seven million Englishmen seeking cheap holidays. Blackpool has the carefree atmosphere of Atlantic City —but remains totally British*

SUN AND SAND (*left*) attract crowds of refugees from rain-soaked cities. But most of them, napping in sight of Blackpool's famous tower, keep well covered up.

SURF AND SEA WALL compete with the beach to delight the vacationers. When visitors have had enough sunbathing and promenading, they brave the gentle waves or ferry out through the shallows in old military amphibious craft to take rides in sturdy motorboats. A fast ride costs two shillings for each passenger, or 28 cents.

8

The Cultural Ferment

THE arts in today's Britain are in a state of immense confusion, internal conflict and rapid change. Their over-all condition, in short, is very much like that of Britain itself. In some ways they show signs of robust vigor. But in other ways they reflect a deep national sickness —the sickness of a Little Britain that is obsessed to the point of aberration with its manifold frustrations.

A newly affluent people's new hunger for a richer intellectual life is evident everywhere. By contrast with the 1930s, when London dominated the nation's cultural opportunities, provincial cities in the 1960s possess some of the finest art museums. There are more full-time symphony orchestras in Britain than ever before, and they are heard in areas that almost never enjoyed live music before World War II. More operas are performed in London than in any other city save Berlin. More new plays are staged in London than in New York; new playwrights and actors are welcomed and encouraged. The number of new books published increases steadily. Britons borrow books from public libraries at the prodigious rate of 450 million copies a year. Radio, television and movies, tiresome though most of their products are, provide ever-growing popular outlets for worthwhile works. Largely inspired by some television programs on archaeology, amateur British diggers are attacking Britain's ancient ruins with unprecedented and fruitful enthusiasm.

AND yet, in this thriving and literate Britain of the 1960s, the worst in British life and the British character sometimes appears to overwhelm the best. Some of the country's most vigorous young writers deride and deprecate the very notion of vigor and purpose in either national or individual life. Many of them treat the postwar rise in general well-being as a curse rather than a blessing—because, among other things, it allegedly makes life dull and unrewarding while making it easier. At a time when many Britons are moving upward socially and economically, a corrosive consciousness of the country's historic class distinctions pervades its fiction and drama. To an extent of which they themselves are often unaware, the practitioners and spokesmen of the arts in Britain thrash against the confines of what a London writer calls "the Little England rut."

Creative genius in any age or land is miraculous, and the British genius of the past bathes the island arts in a golden light. It has always been a genius primarily for the written arts of prose, poetry and drama (which must be written before it can be spoken). For every foreigner with a claim to literacy who is able to identify such great British painters as Thomas Gainsborough (1727-1788) and Joseph Mallord William Turner (1775-1851), millions have at least a nebulous acquaintance with the poetry, plays or novels of Geoffrey Chaucer, William Shakespeare, John Milton, Alexander Pope, Charles Dickens, Jane Austen, John Keats, William Wordsworth, Robert Burns and Thomas Hardy.

The fact that the written arts still evoke and reflect the character of Britain is something of a paradox. No British novelist, poet or dramatist writing today enjoys the world pre-eminence of Henry Moore, an Englishman who has with reason been called "the greatest sculptor of our time." The English composer Benjamin Britten similarly towers above his contemporaries in a way that very few living British writers can be said to do. Modern British painters, ranging from veterans like David Jones (a Welshman of great talent), Graham Sutherland, John Piper and Ben Nicholson to Francis Bacon, whose canvases speak of torment and death, combine craftsmanship with vigor to a degree that is all too rare in contemporary British writing. Yet it is still to Britain's writers, rather than to their fellows of the other arts, that observers must turn for a special insight into the diverse, lively and troubled British cultural scene.

ONE way to sum up Britain's present cultural ferment is to say that it is part and symptom of a great social revolution. This explanation would have it that all of the arts, as well as the standards by which they are judged, are said to be responding to a mighty push from the bottom of the social structure. Viewed in this perspective, Britain seems to have cast aside its traditional class culture and to be reaching for a new "mass culture," cut along egalitarian American lines, to meet the aspirations of a prosperous, educated democracy with the highest literacy rate in its history.

Something of the kind is indeed happening. But it is not happening with the finality that the purely sociological explanations tend to suggest. British society and the British character are too complex, too rich in subtle differences of circumstance and attitude, too enduring in some fundamental respects, for simplified analysis of this sort to be sufficient.

A thoughtful look at the most interesting facet of the changing scene—the emergence since 1950 of successive crops of young novelists and playwrights from the working class and the lowest rungs of the lower middle class—will show just how un-simple and contradictory the changes really are.

First to appear in the mid-1950s were the so-called "Angry Young Men" with their various sour views of postwar Britain and all of its welfare blessings. Playwright John Osborne's flaccid non-hero, Jimmy Porter, set the tone in *Look Back in Anger*: "Nobody thinks, nobody cares. No beliefs, no convictions and no enthusiasm. . . . There aren't any good, brave causes left. If the big bang does come and we all get killed off . . . it'll just be for the Brave New-nothing-very-much-thank-you."

The best known of the "Angries" were Osborne (who also wrote *The Entertainer* and *Epitaph for George Dillon*) and three novelists: Kingsley Amis (*Lucky Jim*), John Braine (*Room at the Top*) and John Wain (*Hurry on Down*, published in the U.S. as *Born In Captivity*). They and several others of their ilk were just getting used to success when a still younger passel of snarlers began to push them out of first place in what might be termed Britain's Futility Sweepstakes. Unlike the original Angries, who seemed to share the hopelessness of their characters, some of the newer people wanted to get something done—although they went about it in very odd ways. Among the most talented of the post-Angries are playwrights Harold Pinter (*The Caretaker*) and Arnold Wesker (*Chips with Everything*). Another one is Alan Sillitoe, who made his mark with a collection of short stories, *The Loneliness of the Long-Distance Runner*, and a rowdy working-class novel, *Saturday Night and Sunday Morning*.

SILLITOE'S lonely long-distance runner, a boy at one of the British reform schools called Borstals, provides a notion of the new approach. In a grimly funny parody of traditional British sportsmanship, the boy describes the head of the reform school and his guests on the day of an important foot race between that institution and competing Borstals: "The pop-eyed potbellied governor said to a pop-eyed potbellied Member of Parliament who sat next to his pop-eyed potbellied whore of a wife

that I was his only hope for getting the Borstal Blue Ribbon Prize Cup. . . . " But the boy throws the race because for him it is the only honest thing to do. Since he just doesn't believe in anything, let alone the upper-class love of sports, except his own odd sense of integrity, winning the race would have been dishonest.

THE backgrounds of the new writers, 'the grubby circumstances and attitudes of the characters in their plays and novels, and the popularity of their work fostered an impression that a new audience for "realistic" drama and fiction had burst from Britain's social depths. This was true only in part. In the affluent Britain of the 1950s, many thousands of people who previously would never have thought of buying a novel above the penny-dreadful level or of setting foot in a legitimate theater suddenly had the money and the inclination to do both. But the over-all result was more a matter of the broad, infinitely varied and relatively privileged middle class expanding downward than of the bottom-most working class surging upward. As *The Times Literary Supplement* observed: " . . . it is a revolution in the taste of middle class audiences who found themselves increasingly drawn to plays which formerly they would have ignored as avant garde, wild cat and vaguely reprehensible." Although many of the new playwrights are from the working class, "they are not writing for working class audiences and their work, in so far as it flourishes, flourishes only by grace of middle class patronage."

One of the working-class playwrights under discussion, Arnold Wesker, has said that he had "a marvelous time" during his very recent boyhood in the slums of London's East End: "I loved it! I was a happy and obstinate little bastard!" But he suffered afterward because the working class displayed so little cultural fervor and so little desire to be uplifted along Wesker lines. "Nobody's listening," Wesker wailed. The central character in one of his earlier plays, *Roots*, is a country girl who returns to her cloddish family of farm laborers after three years of stimulating life in London with an intellectual lover named Ronnie. At the play's climax the girl cries to her deplorably contented relatives: "We don't fight for anything, we're so mentally lazy we might as well be dead. Blust, we are dead! And you know what Ronnie says sometimes? He says it serves us right. That's what he says—it's our own bloody fault!"

Wondrously and, it may be, unconsciously, Wesker expressed in another passage the strange amalgam of envy and something close to wishful love that underlies the characteristic Englishman's attitude toward whatever may lie beyond and above him. "Somewhere in my vision of the world," Wesker wrote in the magazine *Encore*, "I see families living in large Elizabethan type houses, where there are balconies for groups to play music, and act, and where there is room to entertain friends. . . . Surely if it is true that the aristocracy knew and know how to live with grace and dignity and enthusiasm then it is not so much that one wants to do away with the aristocracy as that one wants to see all of us aristocrats, living as dignified human beings with enough time and space to be enthusiastic."

EVEN in its expansive and spacious periods, Britain is a tight little island where the personal lives of those who practice the arts are as much a part of the cultural scene as their work is. Therefore it is natural that the adjustment of the postwar writers to success and acclaim should tell a good deal about modern Britain. No aspect of that adjustment is more revealing than the newcomers' ultimate reactions to that labyrinthian institution, the Establishment.

Perhaps because it exists mainly in the minds of people who are not in it, the Establishment has never been satisfactorily defined. Yet it is a pervasive and potent force in British life. As conceived by the "Outs," the Establishment is a closed community of the "Ins," privileged people with more or less common backgrounds and attitudes. They are supposed to dominate —and to some extent *do* dominate—a variety of fields and institutions which in themselves are also parts of the Establishment. Among them

are the Church of England, the army, the Tory party, certain universities and elite schools, the Civil Service, various organs of the press like *The Times*, and the London financial complex known as "the City."

Among the many subdivisions of the total Establishment, there is of course a Literary Establishment. It includes all of the publishers, writers and critics who have "arrived" and been accepted among and by one another at a given time. When the Angries of the 1950s roared onto the scene, this Establishment or composite "Literary Society" consisted largely of people from middle- to upper-class backgrounds who had been nursed in childhood by "nannies," had attended a respectable public school and Oxford or Cambridge University, and had thoroughly absorbed the standards and atmosphere of "the Gentleman's England."

Among them were many of the British writers who had reputations elsewhere: the incomparable Sitwells (Sir Osbert, Sacheverell and Dame Edith); novelists Evelyn Waugh, Graham Greene and Angus Wilson; poets Robert Graves (who also is a novelist) and John Betjeman; and so on. Those among them who had missed the full treatment in their youth had nevertheless acquired the gentlemanly patina of thought, style and total attitude. Either from actual experience or through social osmosis, practically all of them could say with a writer in *The Times Literary Supplement:* "Our memories are cluttered with nannies, tea under the limes, the sound of [cricket] bat on ball, and witty Oxford conversation."

THANKS to the expansion of educational opportunity that had begun when even the older Angries were young, some of the newcomers had also known the joys of Oxford and Cambridge. But at first they professed a refusal to conform to the pattern of gentlemanly adjustment. It seemed for a time that they were trying to blow away the whole Establishment in the storm of their contempt and rejection.

But not for long. Stephen Spender, a thoroughly established poet, critic and editor put it very succinctly: "England is the country," he wrote, "where the writers meet all the time, know each other completely, and never escape from mutual ingrown self-awareness. . . . The young writer soon finds that the talk about cliques was nonsense; there is only one clique, and he is in it."

NOVELIST Kingsley Amis spelled out the point when he simultaneously announced his happy adjustment to Literary Society and rang down the curtain on the Young Angries. He wrote (in the distinguished London magazine *Encounter*) that "the world of letters, into which I finally contrived to infiltrate, proved benign, not at all in the grip of that 'London literary racket' I had heard so much about before I got there. . . . starting off as a non-affluent non-Etonian without acquaintances in that world, I found it a surprisingly easy one to move about in." As for the original Angries: ". . . one morning the whole shooting-match just softly and silently faded away; and there we all were, reduced to being judged on our merits again. Which ought to be all right, if the merits hold up."

Osborne, objecting in his surly fashion to the acceptance he rapidly won, teamed up with director Tony Richardson to produce several excellent movies (including a superbly acted version of Sillitoe's *Saturday Night and Sunday Morning*). Wesker and Harold Pinter went from success to success, both in London and New York, and the literary press of America noted with envy the proliferation of talented British playwrights for radio, television and stage. British poetry also enjoyed a boom. Philip Larkin, a sometime novelist who was acclaimed by many as the best of the new poets, worked in gently muted rhythms that stopped just short of traditional lyricism. Ted Hughes, growling in verse with animal vigor, held a position midway between the almost-singers of the Larkin school and a mixed bag of lesser poets whose principal characteristic, according to one of them, was their "extreme, almost obsessional, interest in physical cruelty."

The post-Angries were beginning to fade a bit when the literary sociologists, writers who both reflect social change and analyze its elements, came into high fashion. Chief among them were Richard Hoggart, who was born in a slum and became a university professor, and Colin MacInnes, a son of novelist Angela Thirkell. Since the appearance of *The Uses of Literacy*, his brilliant study of the impact of mass media and advertising upon the working class, Hoggart has been accepted as an authority on subjects ranging from the educational system to the right of writers to portray fornication in Anglo-Saxon terms. MacInnes specializes in what he calls "the teen-age thing." In a collection of essays (*England, Half English*) and a wildly funny but also very serious novel (*Absolute Beginners*), he has dissected in masterly detail the minds, talk, habits and concerns of British teenagers. He is the J. D. Salinger of Britain, and his *Absolute Beginners* is often compared with Salinger's *Catcher in the Rye*.

HOGGART and MacInnes may be said to personify the British dilemma. They welcome the pains of social change, believing that something new and good must come of it. But they are unable to define with confidence what that new something may be. For example, MacInnes holds that his beloved teenagers "are the most vital and exciting group around . . . the sharpest, sexiest, most glamorous people we have." In honesty he is then impelled to add: "I'm not wholly with them. I'm afraid there's an awful mindlessness about them. They don't think much, or toss ideas around." On the larger subject of Britain and its prospects, he is at once vague and purposeful. "No one knows what's on," MacInnes says. "But it does get clear that we've got to pull up our socks. Well, that's fine with me. It should be an interesting time."

Among those who made it an interesting time were "the new satirists." They were amateur night-club enterprisers, amateur actors and television producers, amateur journalists; anything, one might have thought, but serious artists. To call much of their work "satire" was to dishonor an honorable term. Yet the new satirists came to constitute an important, if perhaps transient, cultural force. Most of them were very recent graduates of Cambridge University when they burst upon London to open a night club which they called "The Establishment." Its specialties were skits which gave Britons a much-needed occasion to laugh at all that was complacent and stagnant in traditional, upper-class Britain—Establishment Britain. Thriving upon the great truth that there is nothing funnier than a privileged Englishman imitating himself, the night club spawned a string of prosperous enterprises. They included a stage revue, *Beyond the Fringe*, which played to sold-out houses first in London and then in New York; the most popular program on British television, a weekly parody of the news called *That Was the Week That Was;* a scrummy but successful London periodical, *Private Eye;* and a transatlantic version of the original night club. The equal success of the new satire in both countries proved, if nothing else, that Americans enjoy laughing at what Britons need to laugh at.

OF course the newcomers who command so much current attention have not really extinguished the older generation of creative Britons who either were born into spacious circumstances or worked their way there. It often just seems that way. In fact the Gentlemen Writers still outnumber the professional non-Gentlemen and still command more respect and attention abroad than the newcomers do. In perceptive commentary on the world of scholars and scientists, for example, nothing can match Sir Charles Percy Snow's sequence of novels that carries the inclusive title of *Strangers and Brothers*. In what one critic calls his "loving concern with bureaucratic man," Snow is examining the nature of power in Britain, particularly as it brings the scientists into contact and competition with lay officialdom. Some critics question the merits of his writing as writing, but few dispute his insight into the workings and problems of a modern technological society.

Snow gained personal stature in 1962 from the dignity with which he endured a bitter attack upon both his ability and his literary integrity by F. R. Leavis, a famous and acute but acidulous British critic.

Novelist Anthony Powell (pronounced to rhyme with Lowell) is turning out a narrative series called *Music of Time*. His is the England that the Weskers of the 1960s variously deride and dream about: a kind of upper-class Bohemia whose inmates love each other, hate each other, compete with each other and dump sugar over each other as if life could still be fun. Withal, as an English critic has said, Powell ". . . conveys the strict limits of class feeling in [British] society, and at the same time suggests the ways in which those limits are continually being extended and flouted."

There was some evidence that cultural Britain was steadying up a bit. In the booming London theater, the biggest share of the business went not to the new drama of rebellion—though it continued to do very well—but to the revivals of old stand-bys, especially Shakespeare. The new poets throve, as the commerce of poesy goes. But the lyric rhythms of traditionalist John Betjeman (*Summoned by Bells*) and the continually reprinted poems of the Anglicized American T. S. Eliot far outsold the newer verse. One of the literary weeklies reported a shift in the vogue of the new satire: the masses still lapped it up, said the *New Statesman*, but the tastemaking "Ins" were beginning to yawn instead of laugh.

THESE developments were positively offensive to many of the literary newcomers who associated conscious and refined craftsmanship with class-conscious snobbery and with what one of them has called the "vacuous and modish fringe of the literary world." But this was Britain, after all, where in every sphere, but especially in the literary world, change is the only constant. It was certain that the raw and raucous newcomers would one day awake, like so many of their predecessors, to find themselves suddenly on the unmodish fringe.

Benjamin Britten, one of the very few British composers of major stature in 300 years, rehearses with U.S. violinist Yehudi Menuhin.

A New Distinction in the Arts

In a diversity of arts today, Britons' aspirations as yet exceed their achievements. The lively writers born of the national ferment include no Dickens, Byron, Shaw or Strachey, and distinguished painters are rare. But in ballet, music and sculpture, present-day Britain boasts great names. Irish-born Dame Ninette de Valois, by her inspiring direction, made the Royal Ballet, which was formerly the famed Sadlers Wells, a fount of superb ballerinas and original choreographers. In British music, Benjamin Britten has established himself as the best native composer since Henry Purcell died in 1695. Modern sculpture throughout the world has been influenced by the abstract vision of Henry Moore and the rebellious style of the late Jacob Epstein.

CLASSICIST Gilbert Murray (*above*) was noted for translations of Greek drama. He died in 1957, at age 91.

NOVELIST E. M. Forster (*left*), here chatting with the late Robert Frost, won fame with *A Passage to India*.

BIOGRAPHER Lytton Strachey (*opposite*), painted by Henry Lamb, wrote irreverent histories. He died in 1932.

ILLUSTRIOUS PAINTING *was produced in Britain in the 18th and 19th Centuries by such skilled craftsmen as William Hogarth, Thomas Gainsborough and J.M.W. Turner. Their techniques, though no longer influential, are still admired*

HOGARTH, an engraver, achieved fame with his satirical oils. Among the first, painted around 1732, was *A Midnight Modern Conversation*, pictured above.

GAINSBOROUGH, born in 1727, was one of England's first great painters. He called this oil of a future debutante (*right*) *Peasant Girl Gathering Faggots*.

TURNER became a master of the subtle diffusion of light on canvas, as exemplified by this painting of Durham Cathedral (*opposite*), which he did in 1835.

MADONNA IN STONE, protectively resting a hand on the shoulder of her child, is the work of Henry Moore, Britain's greatest contemporary sculptor, who brought to his theme a dignity that is awesome and yet human. A detail is shown above.

MODERNS *in sculpture and painting have restored Britain to high artistic rank*

SURREALISM influences the painting of Graham Sutherland, and though he is foremost in his field, his work often touches off hot controversy.

PRIMITIVISM dominates the massive *Christ* of the late American-born Sir Jacob Epstein. The work was derided when he unveiled it in 1935.

ANGRY YOUNG MEN *of recent literature inveigh against conformism, voicing youth's frustrations in a land they find lacking in challenges*

ANTI-CLASS, John Braine devastatingly analyzed a brash social climber in *Room at the Top*. The son of a city maintenance worker, Braine lives in industrial Yorkshire.

ANTI-SOCIAL, Colin Wilson (*left*) wrote a nihilistic book, *The Outsider*, while camping to save money. His sweater has become a trademark among less successful rebels.

ANTI-CONFORMITY, Kingsley Amis in *Lucky Jim* pictured a lowborn teacher's determined efforts to bluff his way through a small, thoroughly conformist university.

ANTI-SMUGNESS, John Wain (*right*) in *Born in Captivity* described a lively youth's revolt against his conventional, middle-class upbringing. Wain is a dentist's son.

Eyes straight ahead, students at Cheltenham, a girls' school, primly ignore town boys as they stride home from church. They wear the

severe uniform that is common to English educational institutions.

Education:
Mirror
of a Society

THE pace of cultural and social change in today's Britain is illustrated by the odd history of those pregnant words, "the Establishment." The term has a tangible meaning today for just about everybody in Britain who is alert enough to be interested in what is happening to the nation. The fact that no two Britons seem to agree on just what it means only enhances its value as a stimulant to debate and discussion. Briefly, however, the Establishment comprises those influential persons who seem—at least to their detractors—to dominate the political and cultural life of the country. In whatever way it is interpreted, it connotes the attitudes, customs and institutions that are presumed to determine —for better or for worse—the national character and face that Britain displays to the world.

Yet general talk about "the Establishment" started only in 1955. The editor of *The Establishment*, a book of vehement essays on the subject, says in his preface that in 1953 the term "was not in use at all," but a year later it had crept into conversation "among the thoughtful." Then a weekly columnist named Henry Fairlie observed casually in the latter part of 1955 that "the Establishment" had "protected" the treachery of Guy Burgess and Donald Maclean, two British diplomats who defected to the Soviet Union after years of secret betrayal.

Something in the ring and implications of "the Establishment" in this context appealed to writers and other articulate Britons. The astounding zest with which the term was picked up and popularized was in itself a social phenomenon. Within four years Fairlie himself was driven to write: "It is a pity, one sometimes feels, that it was ever popularized . . . the Establishment is now a harlot of a phrase. It is used indiscriminately by dons [university teachers], novelists, playwrights, poets, composers, artists, actors, dramatic critics, literary critics, script-writers, even band leaders and antique dealers, merely to denote those in positions of power whom they happen to dislike most."

THE Establishment derives its abused and indefinable name from one of its principal pillars, the legally established Church of England. Ever since King Henry VIII in 1534 broke away from the Roman Catholic Church and made the Church of England independent, this religious body has been intimately identified not only with the state as such but with the social and economic groups that have dominated life and government in England.

The English church is no longer supported by public funds and special taxes, as it was until the middle part of the 19th Century, but it is still a state instrument in many respects. As "Defender of the Faith" the reigning sovereign is its temporal head and by law must be a member of the established church. All clergymen of the English church must swear allegiance to the Crown, and prayers for the royal family are included in the written services prescribed by law. These services, the canon laws or rules of the church, and its Church Assembly's enactments cannot be changed without the assent of Parliament in some cases and the sovereign in others.

Although its expenses and needs chronically exceed its income, the church is one of England's biggest property owners. Its annual revenue from real estate and other investments is around $44 million, and its total income from all sources, including contributions, is about $100 million a year. Throughout the last century and well into this one, the church was so closely linked to the country's landed and conservative interests that it was once described in a famous jibe as "the Tory party on its knees." The label is no longer completely pertinent, but in the words of an English writer, "it is still usual for people of social position or pretensions to be at least nominal members of the Church of England."

THE all-inclusive Establishment extends naturally from the Anglican Church to the world of graceful leisure. Although the church has recently been broadening the social pattern of its clergy, the characteristic parish vicar has traditionally been—and may still be—a gentleman from the middle or upper classes who played cricket and Rugby at a "good" school and who regards the annual boat race between Oxford and Cambridge Universities, one of which he almost certainly attended, as an event of cosmic importance.

The Establishment plainly owes much of its hardihood to the sheer competence displayed by its members over many generations. But a familiar argument holds that the noblest virtues of these same members were inculcated on the playing fields of England's elite "public" schools. The very essence of the Establishment mentality is embedded in the famous saying (attributed to the Duke of Wellington) that the Battle of Waterloo "was won on the playing fields of Eton." This classic piece of smuggery incorporates several basic Establishment notions which may be summarized as follows: Of course it's the officers and not the private soldiers who win battles. Of course the officers are gentlemen, otherwise they could never have become officers. As gentlemen they of course were educated at Eton or at one of the few other schools in Eton's social league. And of course a rigorous exposure at these schools to games, floggings, Latin and Greek enhances the character of well-born Englishmen and their natural fitness to lead lesser Englishmen in battle and in all other national endeavors.

Traditional Establishment attitudes of this sort are changing, like everything else in today's Britain. For example, "non-gentlemen" who have never been near Eton and conceivably never played cricket can now become army officers. An impressive proportion of Britain's leaders in almost every field, however, *did* attend one of the preferred public schools, and the chances are that those who were unable to do so conceal the fact whenever possible. A "good" social and educational background is still tremendously important in Britain, and it is particularly important in England itself, where the Establishment and all it entails have always been more deeply rooted than in Wales and Scotland.

Lowborn Englishmen can never entirely obliterate the social handicaps that come from being outside the Establishment. This is especially true if their original status is betrayed by their accent, a fact that George Bernard Shaw had in mind when he wrote, "it is impossible for an Englishman to open his mouth without making some other Englishman hate or despise him." There is one route to social and economic betterment, however, that is open to everybody with the mental capacity to take it. This route lies through the schools and universities, and the English youth of today are following it in unprecedented numbers. There they are participating in the most significant revolution in postwar England.

IT is a very peculiar revolution. It is not a revolt against the Establishment and the class system as such. So far as the parents and children who are engaged in it are concerned, it is not a revolution *against* anything. Far from seeking to destroy the Establishment and the associated class structure, the revolutionists are fighting for entry into the Establishment and higher social status for themselves.

About seven million English children—an increase of about two million since 1946—attend some 28,000 primary and secondary schools supported by public funds. Most of these schools are owned and operated by local authorities, but some are conducted by voluntary bodies (such as churches) under official direction. A few supported schools are not under direct official control. Admission to the publicly owned or controlled schools is free; to the others it is partly free and partly at parents' expense. Between them these schools provide an education for all children who want it—and all of the education that most English children ever get. More or less the same arrangement exists in Scotland, Wales and Northern Ireland.

Around 495,000 English children, or about seven out of every 100, attend "independent" schools that charge tuition, receive their support entirely from private funds or endowments and are subject to official control only in the sense that they must meet certain governmental standards. Of these the most famous are the so-called public schools, of which more will be said later.

THE university system may be summarized very briefly: there are two universities, Oxford and Cambridge—and the rest. In all, there are 18 universities in England; one apiece in Northern Ireland and Wales; and four Scottish universities. Britain has nothing quite like the vast American assortment of state, church and private universities and colleges of varying degrees of academic standing. The standard is high at all British universities, which are far tougher than most American ones, the level of study being comparable to that of U.S. graduate schools.

An important and expanding system of "further education" offered in night schools, technical colleges and the like enables hundreds of thousands of young workers who left school in their mid-teens to combine work with continued study. Many employers pay full wages while their workers are at "further education" schools, whether they attend classes one day a week or study for six months at a stretch. This

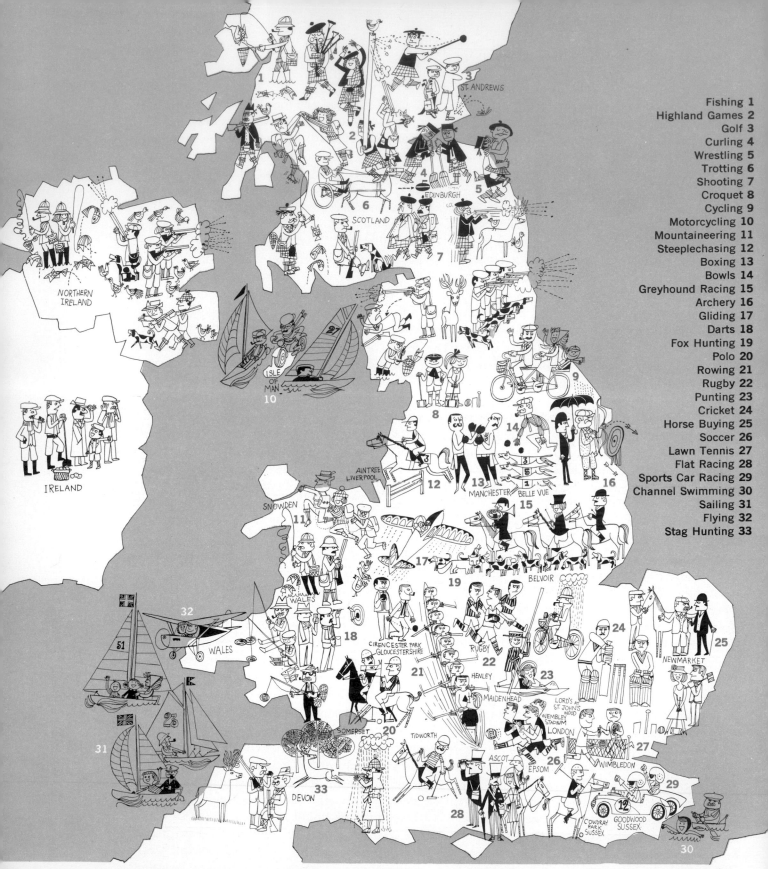

Fishing 1
Highland Games 2
Golf 3
Curling 4
Wrestling 5
Trotting 6
Shooting 7
Croquet 8
Cycling 9
Motorcycling 10
Mountaineering 11
Steeplechasing 12
Boxing 13
Bowls 14
Greyhound Racing 15
Archery 16
Gliding 17
Darts 18
Fox Hunting 19
Polo 20
Rowing 21
Rugby 22
Punting 23
Cricket 24
Horse Buying 25
Soccer 26
Lawn Tennis 27
Flat Racing 28
Sports Car Racing 29
Channel Swimming 30
Sailing 31
Flying 32
Stag Hunting 33

SPORTING MAP OF BRITAIN illustrates the extent of interest in the rugged life, from fishing in the north of Scotland to stag hunting in the south of England. Across the water, the Irish watch the vigorous goings-on in wonderment. To allow inclusion of all of the major forms of activity, the locations given here are only approximate.

148

whole system is founded on the principle that all Englishmen are *not* created equal. An important and frankly acknowledged function of the school system is to distinguish superior from inferior intellect and to educate the children accordingly. The widely held American notion that all children, regardless of ability, are entitled to the same education as a matter of right, at least through the high school level, is beginning to appeal to a number of Englishmen today, but equal education for all is nowhere near adoption as the national philosophy.

FREE public education for all English children began to be instituted in the late 19th Century. Beginning in 1902, schooling was made mandatory for all children between five and 14. In 1944 the minimum school "leaving age" was changed from 14 to 15, and an education through the "secondary" level was guaranteed to everyone. Recently, attempts have been made to enlarge the educational opportunities for those over 15, and 31 per cent of the 15-16-year-old age group has stayed in school. But it is assumed that most children are not equipped to benefit from a university education, and that they therefore will best serve themselves and society by leaving school and going to work.

A series of standard examinations, beginning when children are 11 and continuing through pre-university education, is supposed to separate the academic sheep from the goats and identify children who are qualified for university training. Thus a child's showing on an "eleven-plus" exam largely determines whether he or she then enters a "grammar school" for the minority of academically superior students who may be heading for a university, or goes into one of the "secondary schools" for pupils who are expected to finish their education at 15 or 16 at the latest.

It must be said that England now takes excellent educational care of its superior minority. Regardless of a family's social or economic status, an English boy or girl who qualifies for a grammar school—and about one in every four now does—is assured of all the education that

he or she wants and can justify. For all the children whose parents cannot or do not wish to pay, it is a free education up to 18. Parents of university students must meet a "means test" and pay part of the expense if they are deemed able to do so. But public authorities underwrite all university expenses, including a vacation allowance, of any student who qualifies academically and needs the help.

Nothing like one fourth of England's school-age children take full advantage of the system, however. Only about four per cent of university-age individuals attend universities (compared to 35 per cent in the U.S.), and a program to raise this proportion to five per cent by 1965 is considered ambitious.

The fact that the selection process becomes tougher at every successive stage explains these modest proportions only in part. A far more important reason is rooted in English society. The truth is that even in this time of rising affluence and rising aspiration at all social levels, the *actual* level of general aspiration remains fairly low. It is high only by comparison with what it used to be, and in England until recently it was very low indeed.

A GOOD place to observe something of the educational revolution is the Queensbridge secondary modern school in Birmingham, a prosperous city of just over one million population in the industrial Midlands. "Secondary modern" means that Queensbridge offers both liberal arts and vocational courses for children aged 12 to 16 who have failed to qualify for a grammar school. The school is housed in a handsome, airy structure of red brick and glass, one of about 6,000 new school buildings completed in Britain since 1946. Its 900 students, boys and girls, come from both working-class and middle-class families, but are predominantly working class. Forty of them are Negroes.

When Queensbridge opened its present quarters in 1952, many parents regarded their children's presence there instead of at a grammar school as a disaster. Now the headmaster of Queensbridge, Albert H. Rollason, says there is "much less tendency" to deplore the children's failure to enter a grammar school. The brightest students, once permanently barred from grammar school if they failed at 11, can now try again (though very few do).

But the biggest change, and the one of crucial concern to parents, is that Queensbridge students can now "sit" for the vital General Certificate of Education, a passport to desirable jobs and careers that formerly could be earned only at a grammar school. According to Mr. Rollason, the limit of most Queensbridge parents' ambition for their children is that they qualify for an apprenticeship (training job) in business or industry when they leave school. But more and more Birmingham firms are giving apprenticeships only to those graduates who have earned a General Certificate or its equivalent with good grades, and so the pressure brought by the parents on the school and on their children is formidable.

At the Camp Hill girls' grammar school, a short car ride from Queensbridge, 600 students represent a more ambitious group of parents. Very few working-class girls attended Camp Hill in 1945; now the ratio of working-class and middle-class students is about 50-50. The ordinary "leaving age" at Camp Hill is 16 rather than 15; the test is how many stay for two (and occasionally three) more years in the upper "sixth form," where students may try for an "advanced" General Certificate and perhaps qualify for a university. Ten years ago no more than 35 of the 102 members of a class of 16-year-olds returned to the sixth form. Sixty of the 1962 class returned. Forty of the 100 girls in the 1962-63 sixth form—the highest proportion ever—decided to try for university admission.

DESPITE these expanded opportunities at the state-supported schools, many thousands of English parents pinch their pounds, grovel before headmasters, importune their influential friends and go to any other possibly useful length in order to pay for the privilege of sending off their sons (and their daughters, though in lesser numbers) for a different kind of education. These parents are the patrons and the would-be patrons of the renowned English public schools, which educate about two per cent of England's young men and a far higher proportion of its eventual leaders.

Now almost wholly "private" in every sense of the word, the public schools are so named because originally they were just that—schools for the ordinary and often underprivileged public of the towns where they were founded. Winchester, founded in 1382 as "Seint Marie College at Wynchester," and Eton, established in 1440 by King Henry VI as "the King's College of Our Lady of Eton Beside Windsor," long had more poor students on scholarships than sons of rich aristocrats and landed gentlemen. But increasingly they and others of their kind became—as Sydney Smith, the famous clergyman-writer, described them in 1810— schools "to which the sons of gentlemen resort in considerable numbers."

TODAY the public schools constitute the only sector of English education that has remained relatively immune to change. The "gentlemen," real or self-fancied, who send their sons to public schools today like to think that they do so for the same reasons that Squire Brown, father of the hero of the celebrated 19th Century novel, *Tom Brown's School Days*, expressed when he mused upon why he was sending Tom to Rugby: "Shall I tell him to mind his work, and say he's sent to school to make himself a good scholar? Well, but he isn't sent to school for that—at any rate, for that mainly. . . . If he'll only turn out to be a brave, helpful, truth-telling Englishman, and a gentleman, and a Christian, that's all I want."

In these days of fierce competition for entrance both to the schools and to Oxford and Cambridge (the only universities that most public school graduates want to attend), a modern Squire Brown and his sons have to put much more emphasis on scholarship. So do the schools themselves, many of which have leavened their traditional emphasis on Greek and

Latin with courses in the modern sciences and languages. At their best, the public schools unquestionably provide the finest education of its kind in England and perhaps in the world.

The rampant, plainly sadistic flogging, birching and kindred abuse of students that distinguished the schools of Tom Brown's day have been moderated though by no means abolished. Outdoor sport, while it is still a fetish at many schools, has been somewhat downgraded at a few of them. But an Old Etonian, comparing the Eton that he attended around 1914 with the Eton of today, recently found it "remarkable not that so much but that so little has changed."

An official report some years ago listed 218 public schools. But no more than 90 of these really qualify under one observer's definition in 1899, which still holds good: ". . . an aristocratic or plutocratic [that is, for the merely rich] school that is wholly or almost wholly a Boarding School." Englishmen with a fine sense of discrimination refer to about 20 of these simply as "public schools." (The others are "*minor* public schools," and their graduates suffer all of their lives from the social derogation that the difference in the terms implies.) And among the preferred 20 or so, exactly seven—Eton, Harrow, Winchester, Rugby, Charterhouse, Westminster and Shrewsbury—are the elite of elite.

THERE are a few so-called public schools for girls. But the true public schools, firstrate or shoddy, are for boys from what *The Oxford English Dictionary*, struggling to define these peculiar institutions and their patrons, calls "the well-to-do classes." Perhaps the ultimate tribute to their prestige, influence and durability is this statement by Hugh Thomas, a fervent journalistic foe of the Establishment: ". . . we shall not be free of the Establishment frame of mind, permeating all aspects of life and society . . . until the public schools are completely swept away, at whatever cost to the temporary peace of the country."

In England, much as in the U.S., the pressures of an expanding demand for education finally center upon the universities. It is there that the concept of selective education is under the severest strain, as more and more young Englishmen from the previously under-educated social groups come to regard a university education as their right. How to enlarge existing universities and found new ones without lowering the level of education is the subject of lively debate in Britain.

BUT because Oxford and Cambridge are so profoundly *the* universities, the competitive pressure for admission to them is abnormally concentrated. It is no accident that Oxford and Cambridge are known familiarly as "Oxbridge," a term that sums up for Englishmen everything that is best in university life.

It is possible to say, therefore, that Oxford and Cambridge are too good for their own and England's good. And their predominance has a peculiarly debilitating effect upon England's other universities—vast London University, in a class by itself, and the 15 provincial "Redbricks," so called because, until modern buildings of steel and glass began to rise on their campuses, they were housed mostly in dreary structures of red brick. In such fields as science and sociology, and even in some of the arts, many of the Redbricks are actually superior to Oxford and Cambridge. But all of them are enveloped in a miasma of inferiority that is all the more acute because it is *sensed* rather than observed. Much of what is best and worst in English life and education is implicit in the remarks of two department heads at the excellent University of Bristol.

"I always ask students who want to come to us," said the head of Bristol's English department, "why they don't try for Oxbridge even though our course is definitely superior—for there they will meet the most interesting and promising men and women of their generation. There they will enjoy an exchange of ideas that is impossible here." And the head of Bristol's physics department said, "We've got Cambridge licked—but Cambridge has got something we can never have."

MODERN SCHOOL for primary grades at Doncaster (*left*) is county-run. Such schools are part of an effort to improve both facilities and instruction.

KILTED PUPIL, an eight-year-old Scot of Ayrshire recites the poetry of Robert Burns for his attentive schoolmates. He is the class Burns champion.

The Quest for the Good Mind

Education in Britain began before King Alfred's day and has enjoyed the stature of a noble tradition for some six centuries. But for a long time it was chiefly the privilege of the rich and the aristocratic, who alone could afford the fees of the so-called public schools (which are private) and the great universities. By the start of the 20th Century, however, schooling had become both free and compulsory for all youngsters between five and 14. Most schools are run by local authorities, but some are completely independent.

Scholarships and governmental funds make it possible, at least in theory, for everyone to receive all the higher education that he can absorb. The method of determining who is qualified is controversial and far from infallible. But despite its imperfections, the system does produce, out of every social class, an aristocracy of intellect.

A PUBLIC SCHOOL *since the 14th Century, Winchester emphasizes discipline and classical studies while frowning on social distinctions*

Translating a Latin ode by Horace, boys of 13 (foreground) and

SPIRITED DEBATE amid the statues of the school museum (*left*) explores a possible ban on the Communist party. Students get much training in extemporaneous speaking.

YOUNGSTER'S CHORES include pouring the hot water for the older boys' shaves. By serving others, boys find out what to expect of those who will later serve them.

18 (standing) study together. Some of them read Plato on sight.

EARLY MORNING BATH in cold water (*right*), in a room with a 35-degree temperature, is in Winchester's tradition of a strenuous life, full of hard work and devoid of frills.

STUDENTS AT EXETER fill up a parking lot with their cars as they hurry to classes. Exeter is one of numerous comparatively new institutions established to accommodate the vastly increased demand for higher education. They are called "Redbrick" universities to distinguish them from the austere gray gothic of Oxford and Cambridge.

NOTABLES OF OXFORD gather in the quadrangle of All Souls College for a rare get-together of the heads of the university's 37 independent colleges. All Souls, the Gothic facade of which rises behind the gowned educators, is an unusual college: it has a faculty but no student body. Its active members write and teach in the university.

DISCUSSING AN EXAM which has just ended, male Oxonians chat while a blonde female student anxiously awaits a friend. The traditional gowns denote scholastic status.

The middle-length gown of the young man in the left foreground shows he holds a prized college scholarship. All other undergraduates wear a shorter, sleeveless gown.

IN SOLITUDE, a reader pores over books in the Codrington Library (*right*). Oxonians spend less time at lectures than U.S. students, working more on their own.

10

A Unique and Lasting Strength

PEOPLE in London tell the foreigner who seeks some understanding of Britain, "Whatever you do, don't stay in London. Get out of London and go. . . ." The visitor is advised to go to the villages in Somerset and Norfolk, to Manchester and Stoke-on-Trent in the Midlands, to ancient York and Durham in the north of England, to the coal towns of Wales or to the great cities and wild highlands of Scotland. All of these places and more reveal much of Britain.

But the Londoners who suggest that their incomparable city is like any other capital, distant and divorced from the real life of the country, must know in their hearts that they are wrong. For London contains and projects the whole essence of England, and indeed of all Britain.

One visitor's favorite view of London is from Waterloo Bridge over the River Thames, at twilight on a rainy day. Then the lights and sounds and shapes of the great city are softened and muted in the English mist. Just at the bridge, on the northern bank of the river, is the enormous mass of Somerset House, where every birth and marriage and death in England and Wales is recorded. On Ludgate Hill to the northeast, looming over the original City of London, the noble dome of St. Paul's Cathedral seems to join the low clouds. Hidden in the mist and gathering darkness, but there in the mind's eye, are the squat ramparts of the Tower of London, where William the Conqueror walked and queens of a later time bowed to the headman's ax. As if laughing from across the river at ancient glory and evil, a huge electric sign (advertising a soup) says only OXO. Upriver from the cryptic sign, just west of the bridge, crouches the modern Royal Festival Hall, which Britain built in 1951 to celebrate the postwar revival of its economy and arts.

A dark shaft on the Thames Embankment is Cleopatra's Needle, a granite column hauled from the Egyptian desert and raised beside the river when imperial Britain still took what it wanted from much of the world. Richly glowing above it are the lights of that resort of British and alien plutocrats, the Savoy Hotel. Well up the river, barely visible through the rain, the famous Clock Tower with Big Ben at the top overlooks the massive Houses of Parliament. A shadowy bulk near them is all that can be seen of the grandeur of Westminster Abbey, where Britain's monarchs are crowned.

IT is only a few minutes' walk from Waterloo Bridge to the Abbey, either along the storied Embankment or through the busy street called the Strand. The Strand leads to Trafalgar Square, where the soaring monument to Admiral Lord Nelson often looks down upon crowds of anti-nuclear pacifists and other demonstrators. Nearer the Abbey the stroller is at the very center of British and English public life. For here is Whitehall: the wide avenue of that name and the sooty cluster of government buildings that it also signifies—among them the Foreign Office, the Treasury, part of the old Whitehall Palace where King Charles I was

beheaded and, modestly set off from the main thoroughfare, the prime minister's residence at No. 10 Downing Street.

Although many of its buildings were erected only in the last century, Whitehall looks as if it had been there forever and would be there forevermore. The porters and messengers who preside at the cubicles marked "Enquiries" and guide callers through the interior mazes with ministerial dignity seem to personify all that is sure and solid in Britain. The politicians and civil servants who labor in the offices, often in the comforting warmth of open coal fires, may be handing over the latest piece of freed colonial territory to the natives or striving to preserve Britain's precarious balance of trade. But they somehow embody and convey a feeling that Britain itself is as sound and permanent as the buildings they inhabit.

There is much to suggest that this impression is correct, despite all of the nation's internal stresses and self-doubts.

TO an extent understood by very few people in either Britain or the United States, American investors have gambled that Britain is and will continue to be a sound country. The Ford Motor Company was only following a common trend when in 1961 it bought out (for more than $360 million) the minority British interest in its British subsidiary. Another major car manufacturer, Vauxhall, is a General Motors subsidiary. American investors own more than half of the entire British automobile industry and most of the tire industry. At the latest calculation (for 1961), direct American investment of all kinds in Britain totaled $3.5 billion, equaling about a fourth of British private investment in the domestic economy. The uncertainty over British participation in the European Common Market brought a pause in further American investment, but the stake already acquired was big enough to be a meaningful factor in Britain's economy and future.

In at least one respect American industry takes away from Britain more than it gives. One of Britain's great strengths has been its fund of scientists, technologists and skilled craftsmen. The government has sponsored an extensive and expensive effort to enlarge the nation's human capacity in science and technology. Britons therefore got something of a shock in the early 1960s from the news that around 3,300 of their highly trained scientific and engineering personnel had migrated to the United States since 1957 and that they were still doing so at the rate of almost 600 a year.

This seepage may be due in part to a peculiar handicap that is imposed upon British scientists and men of related skills by their unique society. In every area of intellectual endeavor, for instance, there is a strong tradition of deliberate amateurism, and this extends to British science and technology. Men of immense talent who may devote their lives to arduous scientific inquiry feel called upon to pretend it is really all a game. While this attitude, founded upon the national assumption that only amateurs in any endeavor can be "gentlemen," tends to make life more fun and perhaps stimulates pure science, it somewhat deters the progress of applied science and occasionally even bothers some of the distinguished professional amateurs. Related to this characteristically English difficulty is a feeling on the part of many scientists that they are somehow excluded from the *social* world of the mind, which embraces (or, in their opinion, should embrace) scientists and the better technologists as well as writers and other artists. Esoteric and irrelevant though such a consideration may seem to Americans, it was once the subject of a serious essay (disguised, of course, as an amateur discussion) in that Bible of the Literary Establishment, *The Times Literary Supplement*.

A PARADOXICAL fact in view of all this is that Britain leads the world, including the U.S., in nuclear power plants (operating or under construction) for peaceful use. Two nuclear power stations are already supplying Britain's "national grid" of interlocking power lines. By 1970 Britain will be drawing as much as 10 per cent of its electricity from 10 nuclear stations now in operation, being built or authorized.

In matters of foreign policy, the leaders of both the Conservative and Labour parties act as if the minority of Britons who damn the Western Alliance and call for an ever-smaller Britain were somehow talking about another country. At a point when his prospects for continuance in office were in a decided downturn, Prime Minister Macmillan kept his own and his party's flag nailed to the twin masts of American partnership and total commitment to the Western cause. The new leader of the Labour opposition, Harold Wilson, sought to minimize dependence upon the partnership and to modify the general commitment in some respects. But among his first items of important business was a visit to Washington, to fortify his hitherto casual acquaintance with President Kennedy and to give Americans a set of reassurances that included this statement for the Labour party: "Our position is clear. We stand firmly by NATO and the Western Alliance. We are not a neutralist party and neutralism has no part or place in our policies."

CONSIDERING the unhappy circumstances, the attitudes of both leaders spoke well for Britain as an ally. The ambitious British plans of a few years ago to develop a major nuclear deterrent capacity, including British missiles for carrying British warheads, were just about in ruins. Britain had indeed devised its own atomic and hydrogen warheads, along with a fleet of jet bombers to carry them. But the attempts to acquire adequate missilery had failed technically and also had been found to be beyond Britain's financial means. In the judgment of many American officials, Wilson was making plain sense when he therefore proposed to abandon the whole effort to maintain a British nuclear striking force. But this was only part of a sad and complex story.

Lacking its own missiles, the British government had relied upon the promise that America's experimental Skybolt, which was to be launched from aircraft in flight, would in due course be sold to Britain in sufficient quantities to preserve the usefulness of Britain's bomber fleet (on the theory that the air-launched Skybolts could penetrate Soviet defenses which would in a short time be too much for the bombers themselves). When the Kennedy Administration suddenly canceled the further development of Skybolt, Britain lost that hope of sustaining its nuclear power. At a meeting with President Kennedy in Nassau, Prime Minister Macmillan made a brave show of accepting with pleasure the U.S. suggestion that Britain rely instead upon Polaris missiles, to be mounted in a fleet of nuclear submarines that Britain did not possess and could ill afford.

The crass way in which Skybolt was canceled, as if only the United States were concerned, and the rather patronizing manner in which the Polaris was offered as a substitute, inflamed the already sensitive British people. Harold Wilson reflected their resentment when he declared his intention to reject the Polaris concept when and if his party won office and he became the prime minister.

A GROUP of Liverpool journalists dining with an American visitor bespoke the angers aroused by the Skybolt affair. "We know that Britain's become a kind of backwater," one of the Liverpool newsmen said, "but there's no sense in rubbing it in." The same discussion turned to another source of British bitterness: the fact that President Kennedy had consulted the prime minister only in the most casual fashion during the 1962 confrontation with the Soviet Union over Cuba. "We know Kennedy will do what he has to do," said one of the guests, "but he might show some tact."

This seemingly trivial observation went to the heart of the matter. British foreign policy and British pride since the end of World War II have rested to a considerable extent upon what Britons call their "special relationship" with the United States. Common interests, mutual if not always total affection, and personal communication between American Presidents and British prime ministers have all been elements in this relationship.

Thoughtful Britons had realized for years that it was a relationship of unequal partners. But the same Britons had come to expect American governments and Presidents to minimize, almost to conceal, the inequality. Now, with Kennedy's solo performance in the Cuban affair and the humiliating hop from Skybolt to Polaris, the inequality was on stark display. The "special relationship" survived, as Harold Wilson's care to make a proper bow in Washington showed. But Britons never again would take quite the old pride in it or place quite so much dependence upon it.

BUT the fundamental reason for Britain's sustained sense of national identity and sufficiency is to be found in the quality that has asserted itself throughout this account—in short, in the British character. It has endured and survived far worse trials than the current invasion of American dollars, bomber crews, movies, television westerns, slang and jukeboxes. The most severe strains imposed upon the national character have arisen within Britain itself, among a people adjusting to a loss of power and status in the world community.

Some of the minor reactions to those strains have been ugly, self-destructive and, to many friends of Britain, sorely disheartening. But the total reaction has demonstrated once again that there is a unique and lasting strength in this island people. Losing an empire, they have relinquished it with a wisdom and grace that at least assures them recompense in world esteem. No longer first among nations, Britain remains among the best of nations if the measure is skill in the arenas of power and honor in its dealings (as honor goes among governments).

"Little Britain" is what the country will probably be for the discernible future. But this will be a demeaning status, and will augur a mean and listless future, only if the people of Britain make it so. If they are true to their national character and to the island that has done so much to shape it and them, they will keep for Little Britain a large place in the world's affairs and in the affections of mankind.

At Harwell an atoms-for-peace scientist checks a thermonuclear reaction. Next page: Britons demonstrate against atomic weapons.

A NEW DESTINY *summons the heirs of a severely shrunken empire . . .*

...while skeptical Britons exercise their age-old right to question the wisdom

of the course their leaders have chosen for the march to the national future

Appendix

HISTORICAL DATES

B.C.
700-300 Celtic invasion
55-50 Romans land, led by Caesar

A.D.
5-40 Roman Conquest spreads throughout Britain
62 Suppression of revolt of Boadicea, tribal queen
48-79 Wales conquered, great roads built
410-442 End of Roman era with invasions of Angles, Saxons, Jutes
597 St. Augustine converts Kent and Northumbria to Roman Church
664 Synod of Whitby makes Roman Church supreme throughout England
856-875 Peak period of Danish invasions
871-899 Alfred the Great combats Danes, secures agreement on Danelaw territory
899-979 Alfred's son, Edward, conquers the Danelaw, becomes first true English King
1017-1035 Canute, a Dane, defeats Ethelred the Unready, becomes unopposed ruler of England
1066 Battle of Hastings: Harold, son of Earl Godwin, chosen to succeed Edward the Confessor, is killed by invading William of Normandy
1066-1087 William I centralizes feudalism, requires allegiance to Crown
1106 Henry I conquers Normandy, first foothold in France
1154-1189 Norman Henry II, first of the House of Plantagenet, rules England and most of France; institutes jury trial, fair taxes
1170 Assassination of Thomas à Becket marks rising British opposition to Roman Church
1215 King John signs Magna Carta, recognizing barons' rights
1283 Edward I conquers Wales
1295 Edward's "Model Parliament," most representative assembly to date
1314 Battle of Bannockburn: Scotland secures independence
1337 Edward III's claim to the French throne begins Hundred Years' War
1399 Henry, Duke of Lancaster, ends Plantagenet reign by deposing Richard II
1407 House of Commons wins right to originate money bills
1415 Henry V defeats France in Battle of Agincourt
1455-1485 Wars of the Roses: House of Lancaster and House of York duel for throne

1461 Edward IV of York wins throne
1483 Duke of Gloucester imprisons Edward V, takes throne as Richard III
1485 Richard slain, Henry Tudor wins crown at Battle of Bosworth Field, becoming Henry VII
1485-1509 Henry VII strengthens Crown against barons and lords
1487 Court of the Star Chamber centralizes judiciary under king
1534 Henry VIII instigates parliamentary action abolishing papal rule, making Church of England separate from Rome
1553-1558 Mary Tudor, a Catholic, restores Catholicism as official religion
1558 England loses Calais, giving up last foothold in France
1559 Elizabeth I reinstitutes Act of Supremacy for Anglican Church
1588 Defeat of Spanish Armada opens era of British naval supremacy
1600 East India Company is chartered
1603-1625 James Stuart becomes first King to rule both England and Scotland
1628 Charles I forced to sign Petition of Right broadening Parliament's power
1641 "Long Parliament" dictates severe curbs on royal power; kingdom divided as Charles I rejects series of parliamentary demands
1642-1648 Civil War: Puritans ("Roundheads") vs. royalists ("Cavaliers")
1649 Commonwealth established under Cromwell's lead; Charles I beheaded
1653-1658 One-man protectorate under Cromwell
1660-1685 Restoration of limited monarchy occurs when Parliament offers crown to Charles II
1679 Passage of Habeas Corpus Act
1688-1689 "Glorious Revolution" against James II, who flees to France; crown offered to William of the Dutch House of Orange and British wife Mary
1689 William and Mary approve Bill of Rights defining authority of Parliament
1704 Battle of Blenheim, notable British victory in War of Spanish Succession
1707 Act of Union with Scotland creates Great Britain
1714 George I becomes first monarch of House of Hanover
1720 South Sea Bubble financial panic
1739-1741 War of Jenkins' Ear
1739-1763 Power struggles with France, Spain

1740-1748 War of the Austrian Succession
1756-1763 Seven Years' War (French-Indian Wars)
1757 Clive, at Battle of Plassey, wins French holdings in India
1759 Battle of Quebec: English win Canada; deaths of Wolfe and Montcalm
1763 Peace of Paris leaves Britain dominant in North America and India
1775-1783 War of American Independence
1793-1815 Wars against French revolutionaries and Napoleon
1800 Union of Great Britain with Ireland forms United Kingdom
1806 British annex Cape Colony
1812-1815 War with U.S.
1815 Battle of Waterloo: Wellington defeats Napoleon
1826 Home Secretary, Sir Robert Peel, reforms repressive penal code
1829 Catholic Emancipation Act repeals most legal restriction on Catholics
1832 Reform Bill sponsored by Whig party brings more equitable electoral regulations
1833 Factory Act sets nine years as minimum working age
1837-1901 Reign of Queen Victoria
1839-1842 Opium War: annexation of Hong Kong
1854-1856 Crimean War against Turkey
1872 Secret ballot made compulsory
1875 Disraeli purchases Suez Canal shares; British control canal
1897 Passage of first Workmen's Compensation Act
1899-1902 The Boer War gives Britain control of the Transvaal and Orange Free State
1900 British Labour party founded
1905-1914 Era of liberal reform under Asquith and Lloyd George
1909 Union of South Africa created
1914-1919 War against Germany
1920 Home Rule decreed for Ireland
1926 Severe mining depression and postwar unrest lead to Britain's only general strike
1936 Accession and abdication of Edward VIII
1936-1952 Reign of George VI
1939 Beginning of World War II
1940 Winston Churchill, Conservative, becomes prime minister
1940 Battle of Britain won by RAF
1945 Fall of the Axis powers
1945-1951 Labour party in power
1947 Commonwealth status given to India and Pakistan
1951 Conservatives regain power, Churchill again prime minister
1952 Elizabeth II becomes Queen

FOR FURTHER READING

CHAPTER 1: A COUNTRY OF CHARACTER

Barker, Sir Ernest, ed., *The Character of England*. The Clarendon Press, London, 1947.

Maillaud, Pierre, *The English Way*. Oxford University Press, Inc., 1946.

Middleton, Drew, *These Are the British*. Alfred A. Knopf, Inc., 1957.

Mikes, George, *How to Be an Alien*. Allen Wingate, Ltd., London, 1946.

Nicolson, Sir Harold, *The English Sense of Humour and Other Essays*. Constable and Co., Ltd., London, 1956.

CHAPTER 2: BRITAIN IN THE MAKING

Cam, Helen M., *England Before Elizabeth* (rev. ed.). Hutchinson and Co., Ltd., London, 1961.

Derry, T.R., and T.L. Jarman, *Making of Modern Britain: Life and Work from George III to Elizabeth II*. New York University Press, Inc., 1956.

Elton, G.R., *England Under the Tudors*. Methuen and Co., Ltd., London, 1955.

Green, V.H.H., *The Later Plantagenets: A Survey of English History Between 1307-1485*. St. Martin's Press, Inc., 1955.

Plumb, J.H., *The First Four Georges*. B.T. Batsford, Ltd., London, 1956.

Trevelyan, G.M., *History of England*. Anchor Books, 1952. *English Social History*. Longmans, Green and Co., Ltd., London, 1942.

Wood, Anthony, *Nineteenth-Century Britain, 1815-1914*. Longmans, Green and Co., Ltd., London, 1959.

CHAPTER 3: LITTLE BRITAIN

Allen, H.C., *The Anglo-American Predicament: The British Commonwealth, The United States, and European Unity*. St. Martin's Press, Inc., 1960.

Churchill, Sir Winston, *The Second World War* (6 vols.). Houghton Mifflin Co., 1949.

Franks, Oliver S., *Britain and the Tide of World Affairs*. Oxford University Press, Inc., 1955.

Robertson, Sir Dennis, *Britain in the World Economy*. George Allen and Unwin, Ltd., 1954.

Russell, Bertrand, *Common Sense and Nuclear Warfare*. George Allen and Unwin, Ltd., London, 1959.

Strachey, John, *The End of Empire*. Random House, 1959.

Taylor, Don, *The Years of Challenge: The Commonwealth and the British Empire, 1945-1958*. Robert Hale, Ltd., London, 1959.

Woodhouse, C.M., *British Foreign Policy Since the Second World War*. Hutchinson and Co., Ltd., London, 1961.

CHAPTER 4: THE GOVERNMENT

Amos, Sir Maurice Sheldon, *The English Constitution*. Longmans, Green and Co., Ltd., London, 1938.

Barker, Sir Ernest, *British Constitutional Monarchy*. H.M.S.O., London, 1958.

Bridges, Sir Edward, *Portrait of a Profession: The Civil Service Tradition*. Cambridge University Press, London, 1950.

Jennings, Sir Ivor, *Cabinet Government* (third ed.), 1959. *Parliament*, 1957. *The British Constitution*, 1950. *The Law and the Constitution* (third ed.). Cambridge University Press, London, 1943.

MacKenzie, Robert T., *British Political Parties*. St. Martin's Press, Inc., 1955.

Morrison, Herbert, *Government and Parliament*. Oxford University Press, Inc., 1954.

CHAPTER 5: THE NATIONALLY SUPPORTED STATE

Beveridge, William H., *Full Employment in a Free Society*. George Allen and Unwin, Ltd., London, 1944. *Social Insurance and Allied Services*. B.I.S., New York, 1942.

British Information Services booklets: *Health Services in Britain*, I.D. 735 (rev.), 1960; *Social Services in Britain*, I.D. 780 (revised), 1959.

Kelf-Cohen, Reuben, *Nationalization in Britain*. St. Martin's Press, Inc., 1958.

Robson, William A., *Nationalized Industry and Public Ownership*. George Allen and Unwin, Ltd., London, 1960.

Titmuss, Richard M., *Essays on The Welfare State*. George Allen and Unwin, Ltd., London, 1958.

CHAPTER 6: A WORKING-CLASS FAMILY

Browne, Geoffrey, *Patterns of British Life*. Hulton Press Ltd., London, 1950.

Hoggart, Richard, *The Uses of Literacy: Aspects of working-class life*. Chatto and Windus, Ltd., London, 1957.

Pear, Tom Hatherley, *English Social Differences*. George Allen and Unwin, Ltd., London, 1956.

Scott, John Dick, *Life in Britain: With a Chapter on The English Way of Law by Henry Cecil*. William Morrow and Company, 1956.

Zweig, Ferdynand, *The British Worker*. Penguin Books, Ltd., Harmondsworth, 1952.

CHAPTER 7: THE NEW AFFLUENCE

Britain, An Official Handbook. B.I.S. (published annually).

Lewis, Roy, and Rosemary Stewart, *The Boss: The Life and Times of the British Business Man*. Phoenix House, Ltd., London, 1958.

Lewis, Roy, and Angus Maude, *Professional People*. Phoenix House, Ltd., London, 1952.

Parkinson, C. Northcote, *The Law and The Profits*. Houghton Mifflin Co., 1960.

Rowntree, B. Seebohm, and G. R. Lavers, *English Life and Leisure*. Longmans, Green and Co., Ltd., London, 1951.

Sport and the Community. The Report of the Wolfenden Committee on Sport. Central Council of Physical Recreation, London, 1960.

CHAPTER 8: CULTURE

Dannatt, Trevor, *Modern Architecture in Britain*. B. T. Batsford, Ltd., London, 1959.

Eliot, T. S., *On Poetry and Poets*. Farrar, Straus and Cudahy, Inc., 1957.

Evans, B.I., and M. Glasgow, *The Arts in England*. Falcon Press, London, 1949.

Findlater, R., *The Future of the Theater*. Fabian Society, London, 1959.

Forster, E.M., *Aspects of the Novel*. Harcourt, Brace & Co., 1956.

Haskell, Arnold, *The National Ballet*. Adam and Charles Black, London, 1944.

Rothenstein, John, *Modern English Painters: Lewis to Moore. Modern English Painters: Sickert to Smith*. The Macmillan Co. (Series, 1952-1956).

Summerson, John, *Architecture in Britain, 1530-1830*. Penguin Books, Ltd., Harmondsworth, 1954.

Ward, A.C., *English Literature: Chaucer to Bernard Shaw*. Longmans, Green and Co., Ltd., London, 1958.

CHAPTER 9: EDUCATION

Alexander, W.P., *Education in England*. St. Martin's Press, Inc., 1954.

Judges, A.V., *Looking Forward in Education*. Faber and Faber, Ltd., London, 1955.

Lowndes, George Alfred Norman, *The British Educational System*. Hutchinson's University Library, London, 1955.

Ministry of Education, *Report of the Central Advisory Council for Education in England* (The Crowther Report; 2 volumes). B.I.S. for H.M.S.O., 1959, 1960.

Ogilvie, Vivian, *English Public Schools*. Macmillan and Co., London, 1957.

CHAPTER 10: LONDON AND THE FUTURE

Lambert, Sam, ed., *London Night and Day* (illustrated by Osbert Lancaster). Architectural Press, London, 1955.

Metcalf, John, *London A to Z*. Andre Deutsch Limited, London, 1953.

Mitchell, R. J., and M. D. R. Ley, *A History of London Life*. Longmans, Green and Co., Ltd., London, 1958.

Quennell, Peter, and Alan Hodge, eds., *The Past We Share: An Illustrated History of the British and American Peoples*. Prometheus Press, 1960.

FAMOUS BRITISH CULTURAL FIGURES AND THEIR PRINCIPAL WORKS

MUSIC

Byrd, William	c.1543-1623	Liturgical music: Masses, motets, anthems, services. Songs and madrigals
Purcell, Henry	1658-1695	Opera: *Dido and Aeneas*. Theater music for Shakespeare, Dryden. Anthems, instrumental pieces
Handel, George Frederick	1685-1759	Operas: *Atalanta, Berenice, Serse*. Oratorios: *The Messiah, Samson*. Coronation hymn
Sullivan, Sir Arthur Seymour	1842-1900	Operettas (with Sir William S. Gilbert): *The Mikado, Iolanthe*. Oratorios. Song: *The Lost Chord*
Elgar, Sir Edward William	1857-1934	Oratorio: *The Dream of Gerontius*. Orchestral works: *Enigma Variations, Pomp and Circumstance*
Delius, Frederick	1862-1934	Opera: *A Village Romeo and Juliet*. Chorales: *Sea Drift, A Mass of Life*
Vaughan Williams, Ralph	1872-1958	Symphonies rooted in English folk song: *A London Symphony, A Pastoral Symphony*. Chorales
Walton, Sir William Turner	1902-	Chorale: *Belshazzar's Feast*. *Façade Suite* (poems by Edith Sitwell). Film scores, chamber music
Britten, Edward Benjamin	1913-	Operas: *Peter Grimes, Billy Budd*. Chorales: *A Boy Was Born, A Ceremony of Carols*

PAINTING

Hogarth, William	1697-1764	Satirical moralities: *A Harlot's Progress, A Rake's Progress, Marriage à la Mode*
Reynolds, Sir Joshua	1723-1792	Portraits; frequently experimented with painting techniques. *Mrs. Siddons as the Tragic Muse*
Gainsborough, Thomas	1727-1788	Portraits and landscapes with light delicate air of Watteau, Renoir: *The Blue Boy, Lady Innes*
Romney, George	1734-1802	Fashionable portraits. Noted for grace, elegance of women
Raeburn, Sir Henry	1756-1823	Portraits renowned for simple, direct forcefulness, atmosphere of intimacy
Rowlandson, Thomas	1756-1827	Caricatures, satirical drawings: *Vauxhall Gardens, The Comforts of Bath*
Blake, William	1757-1827	Paintings, illustrations for the Book of Job, *The Divine Comedy*
Turner, Joseph Mallord William	1775-1851	Landscapes, using semi-abstract forms to express forces of nature: *Calais Pier; Slave Ship; Snow Storm; Rain, Steam and Speed*
Constable, John	1776-1837	Landscapes, pioneering in the use of broken color, texture, to create light and motion
Hunt, William Holman	1827-1910	Pre-Raphaelite paintings: *The Light of the World, The Hireling Shepherd*
Morris, William	1834-1896	Paintings, decorations for churches, furniture. Founded arts and crafts movement
John, Augustus Edwin	1879-	Portraits, especially of celebrities: Lloyd George, James Joyce, George Bernard Shaw
Nash, Paul	1889-1946	Abstract painting: *Landscape From a Dream*. Designs, wood engravings
Nicholson, Ben	1894-	Abstract paintings; reliefs in white and gray; cubist and post-cubist geometric compositions
Sutherland, Graham Vivian	1903-	Portraits of eminent figures: Sir Winston Churchill, Somerset Maugham. Poetic landscapes

SCULPTURE AND ARCHITECTURE

Jones, Inigo	1573-1652	Pioneered Palladian architecture in England: Church of St. Paul at Covent Garden
Wren, Sir Christopher	1632-1723	Gave Palladian style full expression: St. Paul's Cathedral, 51 other London churches
Gibbons, Grinling	1648-1721	Woodcarving: choir stalls in St. Paul's, London; Trinity College library, Cambridge
Hawksmoor, Nicholas	1661-1736	Architecture: Christ Church, London. Parts of All Souls and Queen's Colleges, Oxford
Vanbrugh, Sir John	1664-1726	Palladian-style architecture: Castle Howard, near York. Blenheim Palace. Also playwright
Gibbs, James	1682-1754	Model for steepled American churches: St. Martin's-in-the-Fields. Senate House, Cambridge
Adam, Robert	1728-1792 ⎱	Housing group of Portland Place, London; real-estate development of Adelphi Terrace,
Adam, James	1730-1794 ⎰	London, to Robert's plans. Interiors, furniture, decorations
Nash, John	1752-1835	Town planning: Marylebone section of London. Launched neo-classic Regency architecture
Barry, Sir Charles	1795-1860	Leader in use of Gothic revival style: rebuilt Westminster Palace
Epstein, Sir Jacob	1880-1959	Massive, anti-traditional sculpture forms: Oscar Wilde Memorial in Paris, *Day* and *Night* groups, *Jacob and the Angel*. Portraits in bronze
Moore, Henry	1898-	Majestic, semi-abstract sculpture: *Family Group, King and Queen*

LITERATURE

Bede, or Baeda	c.673-735	*Ecclesiastical History of the English Nation* (in Latin)
Bacon, Roger	c.1214-c.1294	Essays: *Opus Major, Opus Minor, Opus Tertium*
Chaucer, Geoffrey	c.1340-1400	*Canterbury Tales, Troilus and Criseyde*
Malory, Sir Thomas	c.1394-1471	*Morte D'Arthur*
More, Sir Thomas (Saint)	1478-1535	Philosophy: *Utopia*
Spenser, Edmund	1552-1599	Poems: *The Faerie Queene, The Shepheardes Calendar, Prothalamion*
Bacon, Sir Francis	1561-1626	Philosophical essays: *The Advancement of Learning, Novum Organum*
Marlowe, Christopher	1564-1593	Plays: *Tamburlaine, Dr. Faustus, The Jew of Malta, Edward II*
Shakespeare, William	1564-1616	Plays: greatest English tragedies—*Hamlet, Othello, Macbeth;* comedies and histories. Sonnets
Donne, John	1572-1631	Poems: *Songs and Sonnets, Problems and Paradoxes, Holy Sonnets*. Sermons
Jonson, Ben	1572-1637	Comedies: *Every Man in His Humour, Volpone, Bartholomew Fair, The Alchemist*. Poems
Herrick, Robert	1591-1674	Poems: *Night-Piece: To Julia*. Song: *Gather ye rosebuds while ye may*
Hobbes, Thomas	1588-1679	Philosophy: *The Leviathan, De Corpore Politico, De Homine*
Milton, John	1608-1674	Poems: *Paradise Lost, Paradise Regained, L'Allegro, Il Penseroso*. Pamphlet: *Areopagitica*
Bunyan, John	1628-1688	Moral allegories: *The Pilgrim's Progress, The Life and Death of Mr. Badman*
Dryden, John	1631-1700	Poems: *Absalom and Achitophel, Fables, Ancient and Modern*. Play: *All for Love*
Locke, John	1632-1704	Philosophy: *Essay Concerning Human Understanding*. Treatises on government
Pepys, Samuel	1633-1703	*Diary, Memoirs of the Navy*
Newton, Sir Isaac	1642-1727	Philosophy: *Philosophiae Naturalis*. Physics: *Principia Mathematica*
Defoe, Daniel	1660-1731	Novels: *Robinson Crusoe, Moll Flanders*. Essays

Swift, Jonathan	1667-1745	Satires: *A Tale of a Tub, Gulliver's Travels*
Pope, Alexander	1688-1744	Poems in heroic couplets: *The Rape of the Lock, Essay on Criticism, Essay on Man*
Richardson, Samuel	1689-1761	Novels: *Pamela, or Virtue Rewarded; Clarissa*
Fielding, Henry	1707-1754	Novels: *Tom Jones, Joseph Andrews, Amelia*
Johnson, Samuel	1709-1784	*The Lives of the English Poets*, a dictionary, essays in *The Rambler* and *The Idler* (periodicals)
Hume, David	1711-1776	Philosophy: *Political Discourses, Essays Moral and Political, Philosophical Essays*
Sterne, Laurence	1713-1768	Novel: *The Life and Opinions of Tristram Shandy*
Smith, Adam	1723-1790	Economic theory: *An Enquiry Into the Nature and Causes of the Wealth of Nations*
Burke, Edmund	1729-1797	*On Conciliation with the Colonies, Reflections on the Revolution in France*
Goldsmith, Oliver	c.1730-1774	Novel: *The Vicar of Wakefield*. Comedy: *She Stoops to Conquer*. Poems, essays
Bentham, Jeremy	1748-1832	Philosophy: *Principles of Morals and Legislation*. Founder of utilitarianism
Sheridan, Richard Brinsley	1751-1816	Comedies: *The Rivals, The School for Scandal, The Critic*
Blake, William	1757-1827	Poems: *Songs of Innocence, Songs of Experience*
Wordsworth, William	1770-1850	Poems: *Lyrical Ballads* (with Coleridge), *The Prelude*, sonnets
Scott, Sir Walter	1771-1832	Novels: *Ivanhoe, Waverly*. Narrative poem: *The Lady of the Lake*. Dean of romantic period
Coleridge, Samuel Taylor	1772-1834	Poems: *The Rime of the Ancient Mariner, Kubla Khan, Youth and Age*
Austen, Jane	1775-1817	Novels of manners: *Pride and Prejudice, Emma, Persuasion*
Lamb, Charles	1775-1834	Essays: "Poor Relations," "The Two Races of Men." *Tales From Shakespeare* (with sister Mary)
Byron, George Gordon, Lord	1788-1824	Poems: *Childe Harold's Pilgrimage, The Prisoner of Chillon, Don Juan*
Shelley, Percy Bysshe	1792-1822	Poems: *Ode to the West Wind, To a Skylark, Prometheus Unbound*
Keats, John	1795-1821	Narrative poems: *The Eve of St. Agnes, Endymion, Hyperion*. Sonnets and odes
Carlyle, Thomas	1795-1881	History: *The French Revolution*. Philosophy: *Sartor Resartus*
Macaulay, Thomas Babington	1800-1859	History: *The History of England From the Accession of James II*. Essays
Mill, John Stuart	1806-1861	Philosophy: *A System of Logic, Essay on Liberty, Autobiography*
Darwin, Charles	1809-1873	*On the Origin of Species by Natural Selection, The Descent of Man*
Tennyson, Alfred Lord	1809-1892	Narrative poems: *Idylls of the King, Locksley Hall*. Plays
Thackeray, William Makepeace	1811-1863	Novels: *Vanity Fair, Henry Esmond, The Virginians*
Dickens, Charles	1812-1870	Novels: *Oliver Twist, David Copperfield, Great Expectations, Bleak House*
Browning, Robert	1812-1889	Poems: *Pippa Passes, Men and Women, The Ring and the Book*. Plays
Trollope, Anthony	1815-1882	Novels: *Barchester Towers, Last Chronicle of Barset, The Way We Live Now*
Brontë, Charlotte	1816-1855	Novel: *Jane Eyre*
Brontë, Emily Jane	1818-1848	Novel: *Wuthering Heights*
Eliot, George (Mary Ann Evans)	1819-1880	Novels: *Silas Marner, Adam Bede, The Mill on the Floss, Middlemarch*
Spencer, Herbert	1820-1903	Philosophy: *First Principles, Synthetic Philosophy*
Arnold, Matthew	1822-1888	Criticism: *On Translating Homer, Essays in Criticism, Culture and Anarchy*. Poems
Huxley, Thomas Henry	1825-1895	Philosophy: *On Races, Species, and Their Origin; Evolution and Ethics*
Meredith, George	1828-1909	Novels: *The Ordeal of Richard Feverel, The Egoist, Diana of the Crossways*
Carroll, Lewis (C. L. Dodgson)	1832-1898	*Alice's Adventures in Wonderland, Through the Looking-Glass, The Hunting of the Snark*
Butler, Samuel	1835-1902	Novel: *The Way of All Flesh*. Satire: *Erewhon*
Gilbert, Sir William Schwenck	1836-1911	Libretti: *The Mikado, Iolanthe*, other famed Savoy operettas (with Sir Arthur S. Sullivan)
Swinburne, Algernon Charles	1837-1909	Verse plays: *Atalanta in Calydon, Tristram of Lyonesse*. Poems: *Songs Before Sunrise*
Hardy, Thomas	1840-1928	Novels: *Return of the Native, The Mayor of Casterbridge, Jude the Obscure*. Poems and tales
Hopkins, Gerard Manley	1844-1889	Dramatic poem: *The Wreck of the Deutschland*. Sonnets
Wilde, Oscar	1854-1900	Plays: *Lady Windermere's Fan, The Importance of Being Earnest*. Poem: *The Ballad of Reading Gaol*
Shaw, George Bernard	1856-1950	Plays: *Arms and the Man, Man and Superman, Candida, Saint Joan, Pygmalion*
Conrad, Joseph	1857-1924	Novels: *Nostromo, Victory, Lord Jim*. Novella: *Heart of Darkness*. Stories
Doyle, Sir Arthur Conan	1859-1930	*The Adventures of Sherlock Holmes*, et seq.
Whitehead, Alfred North	1861-1947	Philosophy: *Science and the Modern World, Essays in Science and Philosophy*
Kipling, Rudyard	1865-1936	Novels: *Kim, The Light that Failed*. Poems
Wells, Herbert George	1866-1946	Novels: *The Time Machine, The War of the Worlds. The Outline of History*. Stories
Beerbohm, Sir Max	1872-1956	Parodies: *A Christmas Garland*. Caricatures: *Rossetti and His Circle*. Novel: *Zuleika Dobosn*
Russell, Bertrand, Lord	1872-	Philosophy: *Philosophy and Politics, New Hopes for a Changing World*
Churchill, Sir Winston S.	1874-	Wartime speeches. History: *The Second World War* (6 vols.)
Maugham, William Somerset	1874-	Novels: *Of Human Bondage, The Moon and Sixpence, The Razor's Edge*. Short stories
Forster, Edward Morgan	1879-	Novels: *A Room With a View, A Passage to India, Howard's End*
Woolf, Virginia Stephen	1882-1941	Novels: *To the Lighthouse, Mrs. Dalloway*. Criticism: *The Common Reader*
Lawrence, David Herbert	1885-1930	Novels: *Sons and Lovers, Women in Love, Lady Chatterley's Lover*
Cary, Arthur Joyce Lunel	1888-1957	Novels: *Herself Surprised, The Horse's Mouth, Not Honour More*
Eliot, Thomas Sterns	1888-	Poems: *The Waste Land, The Love Song of J. Alfred Prufrock*. Verse play: *Murder in the Cathedral*
Toynbee, Arnold Joseph	1889-	*A Study of History*
Huxley, Aldous Leonard	1894-	Novels: *Chrome Yellow, Point Counter Point, Brave New World*. Essays
Greene, Graham	1904-	Novels: *The Confidential Agent, The Heart of the Matter, The End of the Affair*
Snow, Sir Charles Percy	1905-	Novels: *Strangers and Brothers* series. Also scientist and administrator
Auden, Wystan Hugh	1907-	Poems: *The Double Man, The Age of Anxiety*
Fry, Christopher	1907-	Verse plays: *The Lady's Not for Burning, Venus Observed, A Sleep of Prisoners*
Spender, Stephen	1909-	Poems: *The Still Centre, Ruins and Visions*. Criticism: *Forward From Liberalism*
Thomas, Dylan	1914-1953	Play: *Under Milk Wood*. Story: *Adventures in the Skin Trade*. Poems

Credits

The sources for the illustrations in this book are shown below. Credits for pictures from left to right are separated by commas, top to bottom by dashes.

Cover—Dan Weiner for SPORTS ILLUSTRATED

8—Anthony Linck

17—Mark Kauffman

18, 19—William J. Sumits

20, 21—Bob Isear, Mark Kauffman

22, 23—Dmitri Kessel

24—Mark Kauffman

25—Eliot Elisofon

26, 27, 28—Cornell Capa from Magnum for SPORTS ILLUSTRATED

29—Cornell Capa from Magnum

30, 31—Robert Frank except right Henri Cartier-Bresson from Magnum

32—Mark Kauffman

42, 43—The Bettmann Archive—Culver Pictures

44—The Bettmann Archive

45—Dmitri Kessel

46, 47—Dmitri Kessel courtesy The Walker Art Gallery, Liverpool, Dmitri Kessel

48, 49—Larry Burrows courtesy National Maritime Museum, Greenwich—Larry Burrows courtesy Wellington Museum, London

50—Larry Burrows courtesy C.A. Gladstone, Hawarden Castle

51—Larry Burrows courtesy National Portrait Gallery

52—Brian Brake from Magnum

56—Map by Bill Dove

59—Carl Mydans

60—The Bettmann Archive—Reuterphoto from European Picture Service

61—Larry Burrows courtesy The Victoria and Albert Museum

62, 63, 64—Mark Kauffman

65—Brian Seed for SPORTS ILLUSTRATED

66, 67—Keystone Press Agency

73—Carl Mydans

74, 75—Dmitri Kessel

76—Larry Burrows

77—Reuterphoto from European Picture Service

78, 79—Cornell Capa from Magnum

80, 81—Larry Burrows

82, 83—Brian Seed

87—Graph by John Woods

89—John Sadovy

90, 91—Mark Kauffman

92—Camera Press from Pix

93—Carl Mydans— N. R. Farbman

94, 95—Alfred Eisenstaedt

96—Burt Glinn from Magnum, Alfred Eisenstaedt

97—Alfred Eisenstaedt

98, 99—Bill Brandt

104, 105—Desmond O'Neill, Keystone Press Agency

106—Tom Hollyman from Photo Researchers, Inc.

107—Cornell Capa from Magnum —Mark Kauffman

108, 109—Robert Frank

110, 111—Mark Kauffman

118, 119—Alan Clifton, Derek W. Bayes

120—Derek W. Bayes

121—Pierre Boulat for TIME

122—Mark Kauffman

123—Mark Kauffman— Pierre Boulat for TIME

124, 125—Mark Kauffman

126, 127—Leonard McCombe

128—Larry Burrows for TIME

135—Camera Press from Pix

136—Alfred Eisenstaedt— Howard Sochurek

137—Pierre Boulat courtesy Trustees of the Tate Gallery, London

138, 139—bottom left Pierre Boulat courtesy the National Gallery of Scotland, courtesy Beaverbrook Art Gallery, Fredericton, New Brunswick, Canada

140—Mark Kauffman

141—Wide World, Keystone Press Agency

142—Mark Kauffman, David Moore from Black Star

143—David Moore from Black Star

144, 145—Esther Bubley

148—Map by Richard Rosenblum

152—Larry Burrows

153—William J. Sumits

154, 155—Cornell Capa from Magnum

156—Derek W. Bayes

157, 158, 159—Mark Kauffman

160—Jerry Cooke for TIME

165—Larry Burrows

166, 167—Mark Kauffman

ACKNOWLEDGMENTS

The following authorities were of great assistance to the editors of this book: Robert K. Webb, Associate Professor of History, Columbia University; Alan Pryce-Jones, former Editor of *The Times Literary Supplement;* Harold Barger, Chairman of the Economics Department, Columbia University; Henry R. Winkler, Chairman of the History Department, Rutgers University; and Nicolas Bentley, British author and artist, all of whom read the entire book and commented particularly on the chapters in their areas of study.

Index
This symbol in front of a page number indicates a photograph or painting of the subject mentioned.

Production staff for Time Incorporated

Arthur R. Murphy Jr. (Vice President and Director of Production)

Robert E. Foy, James P. Menton and Caroline Ferri

xx

Printed by R. R. Donnelley & Sons Company, Crawfordsville, Indiana

and The Safran Printing Company, Detroit, Michigan

Bound by R. R. Donnelley & Sons Company, Crawfordsville, Indiana

Paper by The Mead Corporation, Dayton, Ohio